Home Office Research Study 227

Middle market drug distribution

Geoffrey Pearson (Goldsmiths College, University of London) and
Dick Hobbs (University of Durham)
with the assistance of Steve Jones, John Tierney and Jennifer Ward

*The views expressed in this report are those of the authors, not necessarily
those of the Home Office (nor do they reflect Government policy).*

Home Office Research, Development and Statistics Directorate
November 2001

Home Office Research Studies

The Home Office Research Studies are reports on research undertaken by or on behalf of the Home Office. They cover the range of subjects for which the Home Secretary has responsibility. Other publications produced by the Research, Development and Statistics Directorate include Findings, Statistical Bulletins and Statistical Papers.

The Research, Development and Statistics Directorate

RDS is part of the Home Office. The Home Office's purpose is to build a safe, just and tolerant society in which the rights and responsibilities of individuals, families and communities are properly balanced and the protection and security of the public are maintained.

RDS also part of National Statistics (NS). One of the aims of NS is to inform Parliament and the citizen about the state of the nation and provide a window on the work and performance of government, allowing the impact of government policies and actions to be assessed.

Therefore –

Research Development and Statistics Directorate exists to improve policy making, decision taking and practice in support of the Home Office purpose and aims, to provide the public and Parliament with information necessary for informed debate and to publish information for future use.

First published 2001

Application for reproduction should be made to the Communications and Development Unit, Room 201, Home Office, 50 Queen Anne's Gate, London SW1H 9AT.

© Crown copyright 2001   ISBN   1 84082 762 9

ISSN   0072 6435

Foreword

This report attempts to describe how drugs are moved from importation to street level in the UK, by whom and for what profit. It represents the first effort to map out the 'middle levels' of the UK's drug markets.

The research is based upon interviews with convicted drug traffickers and law enforcement representatives. The authors find that the middle of the drugs market in the UK consists of a series of interconnected, flexible and relatively small networks and partnerships. These are made up of importers, wholesalers, middle-market drug brokers and retail-level dealers. These networks are regionally disparate yet possess considerable horizontal complexity.

The report argues that there are areas within the middle market where law enforcement agencies could disrupt the supply of drugs in a relatively efficient manner. For instance, it seems that the role of the 'middle market multi-commodity drug broker' may be a strategically crucial link, susceptible to further enforcement effort. Another suggested point of vulnerability is where foreign-based importation groups link with UK-based distribution networks.

David Pyle
Drugs and Alcohol Research Unit
Research, Development and Statistics Directorate

Acknowledgements

The authors wish to acknowledge the helpful contributions of all those who participated in this study. These include members of the various enforcement agencies (Her Majesty's Customs and Excise, the National Crime Squad, the National Criminal Intelligence Service, and various police authorities) who provided interviews and sometimes case studies, as well as the members of other agencies and professions who provided invaluable assistance and information.

We also wish to express our thanks to those convicted offenders who agreed to be interviewed, to the prison authorities who facilitated those interviews, and to others with prior experience of drugs and drug dealing who patiently answered our questions.

Particular thanks are due to Chris Goulden, who was our anchorman at the Home Office. Also to contacts in Customs and Excise, the Metropolitan Police, and the National Crime Squad, who acted as gate-keepers to their agencies and personnel. Many others, who gave us access to their experience and insights into the world of the drugs business, also cannot be named for reasons of confidentiality.

The Drugs and Alcohol Research Unit would like to thank Nicholas Dorn (DrugScope) and Professor Peter Reuter (University of Maryland) for acting as independent assessors for this report.

Geoffrey Pearson
Dick Hobbs

Contents

Summary and recommendations

Introduction and background

The purpose of this study, commissioned by the Home Office, was to improve understanding of the 'middle market' drug distribution system in the UK. The methods employed were tape-recorded interviews with a sample of offenders imprisoned for drug dealing offences and an equal number of personnel from law enforcement agencies (Her Majesty's Customs and Excise [HMCE], National Criminal Intelligence Service [NCIS], National Crime Squad [NCS] and police force drug squads). These were supplemented by interviews with a small number of barristers with experience of drug trials, and some field interviews were conducted with other people with varying experience of drug problems and drug trafficking.

It was decided that where law enforcement personnel were concerned, the aim would both be to gather general information on their understanding of the structure of drug markets, together with specific case studies. By using case studies, it was felt that the information gathered would be comparable to that collected in prison interviews. It was stressed in interviews with law enforcement personnel that our concerns were not with operational matters, rather with mapping drug markets at different levels in the UK.

By these means, approximately 70 usable case studies have been generated, some very detailed. Where the prison interviews were concerned, three-quarters of the sample traded in either heroin or cocaine or both drugs. Equally important in terms of middle market drug distribution systems is that almost two-thirds traded in one substance only.

Key findings

In common with other forms of commodity market, drug markets consist of inter-connected levels of brokerage and transactions involving intermediaries. There is, however, no readily available, nor agreed, definition of what constitutes the 'middle market' in drug distribution systems, nor at which level the 'middle' is located.

Definitions

Different interpretations of the middle market are set out in the introduction to this study. The research focussed mainly on criminal networks and individuals operating within the sphere of activity that lies between bulk importation traffickers/wholesalers and retail level dealers. Even so, these conventional distinctions are often blurred.

Small and flexible networks

Although drug markets are hierarchical, in that transactions involve market-defined roles of responsibility, risk and reward, they are also highly flexible with the possibility for roles of supplier and buyer to be interchangeable at wholesale and middle market levels.

Criminal networks involved in middle market drug distribution are typically small, with a correspondingly small number of suppliers and customers. The notion of organised crime groups as tightly organised, complex and hierarchical entities whose tentacles reach around the globe is not supported by our evidence. They are more usefully understood as networks or partnerships of independent traders or brokers.

Hierarchies and supply chains

A four-tier classification of drug markets is proposed: importers, wholesalers, middle market drug brokers and retail level dealers. These are not meant as rigid categories, since, as stated above, roles can be interchangeable. Nor does it imply that there are always and only four links in the supply chain, since some individuals occupy dual roles (e.g. import and wholesale), while middle market drug brokers are sometimes known to collect and import drugs from wholesale storage systems in continental Europe. At other times, there are numerous linkages and intermediaries. However, the four-tier classification is a simple and usable definition of distinctive market roles and functions.

The number of links in the chain between importation and retail level distribution is sometimes surprisingly short and, in the conventional shorthand of hierarchical pyramid dealing, the market is therefore best understood as a flat or shallow pyramid.

Middle market drug brokerage

The *middle market multi-commodity drug broker* is identified as occupying a strategic position that links upper (importation and wholesale) and lower (retail) levels of the market.

If the vertical dimension of the market is relatively simple and shallow, involving few links in the chain, the middle market drug broker's sphere of operation involves considerable horizontal complexity in terms of how wholesale suppliers are linked to multiple retail-level customers (See Figure 1).

Some middle market drug brokers trade in all the main illicit substances – heroin, cocaine, amphetamine, ecstasy and cannabis. Others deal in only the 'dance drug' constellation of amphetamine, ecstasy and occasionally cocaine. Nevertheless, through their multi-commodity brokerage, they link what are essentially mono-commodity supply chains above them to retailers who are also equally likely to deal in a more limited range of substances.

Middle market multi-commodity drug brokerage networks are typically small: one, possibly two people, who control finances and have established contacts, with a small team of runners working to them who collect and deliver quantities of drugs. Some runners are employed on a weekly wage basis; others are paid per transaction, while others are effectively junior partners in the enterprise.

Regional variations

There are regional variations in drug markets but these are not well understood either in terms of fluctuations in availability or how these interact with local and regional variations in drug preferences and demand. There is not so much a national drugs market, as a series of loosely interlinked local and regional markets. Our research, being of an innovative and pilot nature, cannot claim full regional and inter-regional representation.

Cross-regional networks are also in evidence, although the main basis of drug dealing operations probably remains local and regional.

European links and networks

There is some evidence of middle market drug brokers making direct contact with intermediaries to warehousing systems in mainland Europe and importing modest loads on that basis, thus leap-frogging more traditional systems of bulk importation and wholesale trade. However, this trend is not well understood and could therefore be one focus for future research.

Kinship and ethnicity

The role of kinship and ethnicity in drug networks remains important, in that these are the traditional sources of trust in non-legal (that is, criminal) business enterprise. Hence, the typical 'family firm' still has local importance in some serious crime networks, and various ethnic groups are linked by origin and kinship to source countries for drug cultivation and production, and to traditional smuggling routes.

Nevertheless, market principles require that crime networks reach beyond these narrow and traditional means of securing and enforcing trust. Numerous cross-ethnic network linkages are evident. Kinship and ethnicity might therefore be declining in importance in some aspects of drug brokerage, while possibly remaining vitally important at transnational levels.

Price and purity

Indications of the economic organisation and price structure of different commodity markets are presented in the report.

There is no systematic evidence in the UK on either price or purity structure at different levels of drug markets. Local reports are separately collated by HMCE and NCIS, largely for internal use, but there is no agreed research standard for either reporting or recording. This knowledge gap limits understanding of market dynamics such as profit margins and economic vulnerabilities.

However, on the available evidence, it is clear that street prices are not a valid performance indicator of the effectiveness of enforcement efforts at interception levels. Increases in prices at importation and wholesale levels can sometimes be identified as a result of successful high-level interception operations, but these costs are absorbed and not passed on to the consumer.

Violence in the middle market

The potential for violence runs like a thread through drug networks. However, its nature and significance is often misunderstood and overstated.

People who become involved in the drugs middle market often come with a previously established reputation for violent conduct earned in other spheres, such as those of bouncers and doormen, robbery, or football hooliganism.

Business principles are predominant in the potentially lucrative drugs market, which means that 'violence-avoidance' is the more general rule. Violence attracts attention and is 'bad for business'. Violence is most usefully understood as a consequence of market dysfunction and disorganisation.

Little evidence is found for so-called 'turf wars'. Where these do occur, they appear to be essentially local affairs. Geographical territory seems not to be important in the UK drug market, although 'market territory' (in terms of level of involvement) might be more significant.

Where violence most usually occurs in the drug trade, it is essentially instrumental, to secure contract compliance or to enforce debt collection, and sometimes takes the form of kidnap and torture that often goes unreported.

Recommendations: policy and practice

This is a relatively short-term, preliminary research project, and caution should be exercised in reaching policy and practice recommendations. There are, nevertheless, a few worthy of mention.

Resource issues, perhaps predictably, surfaced repeatedly in interviews with enforcement personnel. This was not so much a question of overall resources, as how to allocate priorities within existing ones. In some regions, notably London, views were expressed that anti-drug enforcement efforts were comparatively under-resourced. Estimates offered by enforcement personnel in London and elsewhere indicated that available intelligence information could support a five-fold increase of operational capacity against heroin dealing, for instance.

A related matter concerned the perceived drift 'up-stream' of anti-drug enforcement efforts, with the risk of leaving a 'void' in lower and middle-levels of intelligence and policing. Given the time constraints of our study, it would be over-hasty to claim that the existence of this 'void' is generalised and universal. We can only register here the anxieties expressed in interviews on several occasions, and the need for more scrutiny of this issue.

The absence of reliable purity data has already been mentioned. It is recommended that systematic purity-testing of drugs seized at all levels of the market will offer improved understanding of the economic structure and vulnerabilities of UK drug markets.

The systematic use of more sophisticated methods of forensic analysis of seized drug samples (gas chromatography analysis, otherwise known as chemical profiling or chemical fingerprinting) could also make a significant contribution to drugs intelligence. These forensic methods are employed currently only at importation level. Paradoxically, systematic fingerprinting of seizures in the middle market and at lower (ounce) levels could identify blind-spots in high-level intelligence and interception efforts.

Future research indications

The middle market drugs business is an area worthy of future research investment. As described in the introductory chapter, there are only a handful of research reports that relate to upper- and middle-level drug dealing, and most of these are American. The UK and USA drug markets share some similarities, such as regional variations, but in other respects they are quite distinct.

We do not recommend reliance on prison interviews on the present model. These are time-consuming and costly to arrange, and often wasteful when it is discovered on arrival for a pre-arranged visit that the prisoner has been moved. Some interviews undoubtedly produced valuable insights, and overall provide evidence for consistent patterns in drug-dealing operations. The quality of information yielded by both types of interviews, however, was highly variable. It is possible, nevertheless, that improved methods of targeting potential interviewees could generate more consistently useful information.

A major way to improve the focus would be to allow sufficient time within any research project for repeat interviews with both enforcement personnel and offenders, where initial contacts are promising. It would also be helpful to target offenders to be interviewed on the basis of recommendations from law enforcement agencies in terms of the type and level of crime network that offenders were involved in. Our experience suggests that the type and length of sentence received by an offender is not a useful guide to the actual extent and level of their involvement in drug markets.

Any future research in this area should adopt a modified and more focused research strategy, of which the following are options.

- A central focus would be what we have identified as *middle market multi-commodity drug brokers* who operate at a strategic level between upper and lower levels of drug markets.

- A second consideration would be comparative studies of inter-city and regional variations in systems of drug brokerage.

- Of equal importance is the level and quality of the involvement of UK-based middle market drug brokers in direct trade with European-based warehousing systems.

- One final possibility would be a network analysis of how the experience of imprisonment contributes to the development of an individual's expertise and cross-regional contacts in terms of the development of drug distribution systems. The importance of prison in generating drug networks was so much of an undercurrent in our research that we suggest that an investigation of this phenomenon could yield valuable data concerning the proliferation of knowledge contacts and pragmatic skills and competencies beyond the local parameters within which most crime networks are perceived to operate. We suggest that, after consultations with law enforcement personnel and immersion in specific cases, researchers could then interview offenders with a view to tracing the trajectories of individual careers and the dynamics of illegal enterprise.

1.

Introduction: background and methods

Drugs are commodities, bought and sold like any others, albeit within illicit markets. There is a vast body of research concerning such matters as the medical and social dimensions of drug use, the characteristics of drug users, the determinants of patterns of drug consumption, and the effectiveness of treatment measures. And yet, compared with the level of research-based evidence on the demand side, there is relatively little research on the supply side of illicit drug markets – whether in terms of the social organisation of crime networks involved in drug trafficking, the economic structure of drug markets, or the effectiveness of law enforcement efforts. This is particularly true in the United Kingdom where the evidence base concerning drug dealers, as opposed to drug users, has for some years been noticeably underdeveloped (Pearson, 1990 & 1991).

This study is one of a number being funded by the Home Office to begin to remedy this difficulty. Our focus is on the social organisation of crime networks operating within middle market drug distribution in modern Britain. This concerns such things as the size and membership of such networks, the division of labour within them, their business relationships with customers and suppliers, and the management of trust and order within illicit markets. Although we have some evidence on the prices of different drug commodities at different levels of the market, this is not an economic analysis of drug markets (cf. Wagstaff and Maynard, 1988; MacDonald and Pyle, 2000; Reuter and Kleiman, 1986). In summary, it is a contribution to the criminological and sociological understanding of middle and upper-level drug dealing.

Previous research on drug dealing

There is very little research on drug dealing in the middle-to-higher range that is relevant to this study. The vast bulk of existing research on drug dealing is from the USA, and most of this is concerned with retail or 'street level' dealing. References to those previous research studies that have most relevance can be found in the bibliography.

Even internationally, there are only a handful of studies that are clearly focused on middle and upper level dealing. Patricia Adler (1985 & 1992) conducted an ethnographic study of an upper-level dealing and smuggling community in California, which provided a quite unique and detailed account of the social networks and lifestyles of people involved in the illicit markets for cocaine and cannabis in the late 1970s. Peter Reuter and John Haaga (1989) some years later produced what they describe as an 'exploratory study' of high-level drug markets in the USA. This was based on interviews with convicted offenders, which, although it provided many useful insights, was not carried forward because of non-compliance of interviewees.

The study by Reuter and Haaga was undoubtedly closest to our own in terms of research methods, although we were more fortunate in the degree of cooperation that we obtained from imprisoned interviewees. Finally, there is a relatively small-scale study, based on interviews with prisoners and registered informants by Nicholas Dorn and his colleagues (1998), which provides a qualitative study of convicted smugglers and risk-avoidance strategies. An earlier study (Dorn et al., 1992) had also offered some brief case studies of middle-level drug dealing. We can also note two projects with some relevance to our own: an Australian research study of convicted drug dealers offers some indications of different market levels (Ovenden et al., 1995), and an ongoing Canadian study of 'wholesale' traffickers which also involves interviewing convicted offenders (DesRoches, 1999). Finally, there is a very recent account of a single drug dealing network in New York, based on the analysis of intercepted telephone conversations (Natarajan, 2000).

By any standards, this is not a well-developed research field, amounting globally to no more than six studies of the mid-to-upper reaches of drug markets. As already noted, there is considerably more research on retail level, or street level, drug dealing, although again this tends to be North American. Some of this available research is concerned with drug dealers who occupy a somewhat ambiguous position in terms of market level. Namely, high-volume dealers who nevertheless operate as sellers directly to drug consumers at retail-level – either as individuals or as teams (Curcione, 1997; Jacobs, 1999; Williams, 1989). Whether these should be classed as 'middle-level' dealers is unclear. Research on drug use and patterns of drug purchasing around the London club scene suggests similar kinds of ambiguity (Ward and Pearson, 1997).

Other research has identified drug dealers who move between different levels of operation, in terms of quantities bought and sold (Murphy et al., 1990; Adler, 1985) and our evidence also points to individuals who occupy different roles and different market levels at different times. Johnson et al. (1992) offered a typology that distinguished ten drug dealing roles at different levels of the market, indicating how these approximate to equivalent roles in conventional markets for licit commodities. There are, however, few if any studies that are concerned with market practices at different levels or with the techniques of dealing. Although Jacobs (1992, 1996 & 1999) has offered indications of how USA street-level crack dealers attempt to avoid enforcement measures, and elsewhere there is an intriguing discussion of the role of developments in telephone technology in facilitating drug dealing (Natarajan *et al.*, 1995).

Turning to British work, there is a limited amount of empirical research on 'dealing' – that is, the purchasing and selling of illicit drugs – and it is almost entirely concerned with the retail market (Lewis *et al.*, 1985; Power *et al.*, 1995; Edmunds *et al.*, 1996; Ward and Pearson, 1997; Pearson, 2001). The exception is the work already cited by Dorn *et al.* (1992 & 1998), which is concerned with higher levels of dealing operation.

In conclusion, the evidence base on drug dealing in general and middle-level drug distribution in particular is considerably underdeveloped. In this context, our own study of middle-level drug distribution must be considered both path-breaking and provisional. We must stress the modest scale of the operation, involving little more than six months of field study, and as a consequence some of our findings should be regarded as tentative. Nevertheless, the research does help us to advance our understanding of some aspects of the middle market, and suggests that further investment in this field would be beneficial.

Selecting research methods

It had been pre-determined by the Home Office that the appropriate methodology for this study was to conduct interviews with 50 offenders imprisoned for drug supply offences, and with an equivalent number of police and customs officers with experience of intelligence and operational matters relevant to middle market drug dealing. Interviewees were selected from lists of both prisoners and enforcement personnel supplied by the Home Office, who had been notified as individuals with relevant experience. Two full-time research workers were employed over a six-month period to arrange and conduct the prison interviews. Experience in the field also indicated that highly suitable candidates for interview could be identified by the prison authorities themselves, or by drug teams working in the prison system.

In one of the few previous research studies into higher-level drug markets, Reuter and Haaga (1989) conducted interviews with imprisoned offenders, as we have done in this study. Quite apart from the lack of compliance among interviewees, the authors drew attention to other shortcomings in this methodology, such as the possibility that dealers might either downplay or exaggerate their roles in drug markets. We will address these problems below.

Criminologists have often based research studies around interviews with convicted offenders. For many years they have also been aware of the potential limitations of prison interviews. As far back as the 1960s, Polsky (1967 & 1998: p. 115) criticised the reliance on interviews in non-natural settings where compliance might be forced or only partial. More recently, Wright and Decker (1997: p. 4) in their study of active armed robbers, have also stressed the value of ethnographic fieldwork as against retrospective interviews with imprisoned offenders in an environment that is far removed from that in which crimes are actually committed.

In terms of the selection of research methods, however, there are very real limitations where middle and upper-level drug dealing is concerned. Ethnographic field research has been employed successfully on numerous occasions in the study of low-level drug dealing and street markets (Bourgois, 1995; Dunlap et al., 1994; Jacobs, 1999; Johnson et al., 1985; Maher, 1997; Mieczkowski, 1990 & 1994; Pearson, 1993 & 2001; Power, 1989; Power et al., 1996; Preble and Casey, 1969; Williams, 1989). Even so, there are important considerations of safeguarding the personal safety of researchers engaged in this kind of work (Williams et al., 1992).

However, the use of ethnographic methods is rarely feasible in the study of upper and middle-level trafficking owing to the degrees of secrecy and security that are employed. Adler (1985) is one of the few researchers to have conducted ethnographic research into upper-level trafficking, and even though her access was highly privileged through a friendship that she had struck up with one of the traffickers, she nevertheless regarded it as risky and imperfect (ibid.: pp. 17-26).

An alternative and innovative approach to the study of a higher-level drug dealing has recently been demonstrated by Natarajan (2000) who conducted a network analysis of wire-tapped telephone conversations that had been recorded as part of a police operation against a drug trafficking organisation in New York. Network analysis has been employed previously in the study of criminal organisations, although its potential is possibly undeveloped (Berkowitz, 1982; Wasserman and Faust, 1994; Ianni and Ianni, 1990; Baron and Tindall, 1993; Sparrow, 1991; Coles, 2001). Even so, there are obvious difficulties in terms of confidentiality and security. Natarajan also observes that the information requirements of social scientists differ from those of enforcement agencies. The information collected and put forward by enforcement agencies is, understandably, tailored to the evidential needs required to secure a prosecution, rather than to the social scientific analysis of an organisation. Furthermore, he suggests that successive developments in communication technology quickly render such forms of intelligence gathering and analysis obsolete (cf. Natarajan et al., 1995).

Conducting prison interviews: the present study

In conclusion, we can say that no form of methodology will be entirely satisfactory when dealing with clandestine activities and organisations. We are satisfied, nevertheless, that the prison interviews conducted in our own study yield sufficient valid information to allow us to generate a sizeable number of case studies that throw light on middle-level drug markets in modern Britain.

We were surprised by the low level of refusals encountered, compared with Reuter and Haaga's (1989) experience, where the participation rate was less than 50 per cent and varied considerably between different prison facilities. A much more serious difficulty in our study was either accessing the administrative systems of prisons, or for the research worker to arrive at a prison only to discover that the prisoner had been moved elsewhere some time ago and could not be traced.

However, once a method had been devised for ensuring that someone with sufficient seniority within a prison took responsibility for a request for an interview to be forwarded to the prisoner, no refusals were encountered. As already indicated, members of prison drug teams could also be extremely helpful in identifying and securing interviews with prisoners who had relevant experience. On two occasions, nevertheless, interviewees denied any knowledge of drug trafficking, and these cases were removed from the analysis. In another three cases, the individuals concerned said that they had been only very marginally involved. Nonetheless, these interviews were found to be useful since they threw light on the sometimes exploitative nature of these relationships in which people are considered to be expendable as bit-part players or as couriers and 'mules'.

In the vast majority of these interviews, although they varied in quality and depth, interviewees were cooperative in different measures and in only two cases did they refuse to allow the interview to be tape-recorded. One check on reliability was the individual's command of drug prices at different levels of the market, and although some involved in courier and transport roles did not know the prices and quantities of the drugs they were handling, those who did tended to fall within an agreed range of reliability. There were one or two occasions when an individual gave a price indication that was out of line, and were either offering an ill-informed speculation or claiming some knowledge and authority that they did not have, but these were easy to identify.

In addition to the prison interviews, a number of field interviews were arranged with people who had various kinds of experience of drugs and drug markets. These were recruited through drug service agencies and other community contacts. They helped to round out our understanding of some points of detail, such as issues of price and purity in the cocaine and amphetamine markets, domestic and small-scale cannabis growing technologies, and the street price of heroin, which has fallen steeply in some parts of the country. A number of these contacts were short and conducted by telephone, but in seven cases they resulted in detailed face-to-face interviews that were tape-recorded and transcribed. As a result, these seven cases have been included in the data presented below on the prison interview sample.

Characteristics of the prison sample

The sample of prisoners generated by the above means was predominantly male and white. Of the 51 completed prison interviews, five were with women (10 per cent) and in terms of ethnicity 80 per cent of the interviewees were white-British. Of the remainder, two interviewees were of African-Caribbean descent and two were of South Asian descent. There was one interviewee of Turkish origin, one Dutch national, one other European national, based in Holland, a white South African, and a Canadian.

In terms of their ages, interviewees were mainly in their late twenties and thirties (Table 1.1).

Table 1.1: **Age structure of the prison sample**

Age	20-24	25-29	30-34	35-39	40-44	45-49	50-54	55-59
Percentage	4%	22%	28%	22%	2%	15%	4%	2%

Offenders varied in terms of their regional sphere of operation, although this could often not be clearly defined. Depending on the level at which they operated, the customer base of some individuals, or their associates, was cross-regional. Their supplies of drugs also often came from elsewhere within the UK, if not directly imported from other countries by their own network or immediate associates. In one case, for example, a man operating as an ounce dealer in an East Midlands city bought quantities of cocaine from contacts in London, while his heroin supplies came from a Merseyside connection. In another case, a middle market heroin broker in Bristol supplied to members of his network in Southampton, London and Manchester. In a third case, a network located in West Yorkshire had both a local customer base for ecstasy, as well as supplying dealers in Glasgow and Manchester, and receiving regular supplies from intermediaries in London, and also importing direct from the Netherlands. Finally, we can note a man who, although he was living in the West Country, supplied drugs mainly to members of the travelling community, so that his regional base of operations was necessarily migrant and transitory.

Where individuals had at some time been directly involved in the importation or exportation of drugs (11 cases), it was also not always possible to be precise in terms of their UK regional location. Among those involved in importation, for example, even where this involvement had been frequent and sustained (7 cases), not all were aware of the destination of imported drugs since they only controlled the transport system and supplied to a middleman buyer. Nevertheless, Table 1.2 provides an approximate indication of the regional sphere of activity.

Table 1.2: **Regional location of the prison sample**

Region	
London and South East England	30%
South West England	18%
Midlands	10%
North West England	16%
North East England	8%
Wales	6%
Scotland	12%

A related difficulty is defining at what level people operated in the drugs market. This was partly because people often moved between different levels during their drug dealing careers. Also, someone might occupy a relatively minor role within a high-level operation – as with drug couriers or 'mules' in transnational systems of importation, or 'runners' within regional or cross-regional distribution systems. However, Table 1.3 indicates the highest level at which an individual might have operated at any one time.

Table 1.3: **Level in the drug market of the prison sample**

Market level	
Import/export	20%
Production	5%
Regional distribution	30%
Local/city-wide distribution	45%

Finally, we turn to the types of drugs in which individuals, and their associates, traded. Here, it is once again difficult to offer a precise summary, since, to some extent, drug markets reflect patterns of poly-drug use among drug users. This does not mean that drug dealers are opportunistic, and are prepared to buy and sell any drugs according to supply and demand. On the contrary, drug markets seem to be highly segmented and patterns of drug dealing form around recognisable clusters of different substances.

The typology that we have adopted is as follows:

- One commodity cluster comprises the so-called 'dance drugs', and middle market dealers are commonly encountered whose business centres on ecstasy and amphetamine, some of whom are also selling smaller amounts of cocaine. In the typology that we offer below, it seems sensible to distinguish between these two sub-types of 'dance drugs' dealing.

- There are also middle market dealers whose central business is in cocaine, either in powder form or 'crack'/'rock' form, and for some this is their sole line of business.

- An even more substantial proportion of our sample was involved solely in the heroin trade, although there are some who sold both heroin and cocaine, including its crack form. Once again, our typology distinguishes between these two sub-types.

Overall, 47 per cent traded in heroin either as mono-commodity dealers or in tandem with other drugs and a further 38 per cent were involved in the cocaine market. So that three-quarters of our sample traded in heroin, cocaine, or both drugs.

This was, of course, a consequence of our attempt to target interviews on heroin and cocaine trafficking, which form a major focus of the UK national drugs strategy. Nevertheless, we felt that it was important to gather some evidence on other aspects of drug markets, such as those serving forms of recreational drug use including the 'dance drugs' and cannabis. Our evidence, summarised in Table 1.4, suggests that those who sell 'dance drugs' invariably refuse at this level of the market to deal in heroin. In addition to the combination of amphetamine and ecstasy, with or without cocaine, they will also sometimes deal in cannabis.

The bulkiness of cannabis and its relatively low profitability, however, mean that this decision is governed by factors other than customer demand. Indeed, the availability of cannabis is spread somewhat unevenly across the different supply clusters set out below and we have identified only those offenders interviewed who were cannabis-only dealers – most of whom were operating at the level of wholesale, regional distribution, or production.

Table 1.4: Types of drugs traded by the prison sample

Drug types	
'Dance drugs' (amphetamine, ecstasy)	15%
'Dance drugs' plus cocaine	11%
Cocaine only	11%
Cocaine and crack only	4%
Heroin only	36%
Heroin plus cocaine/crack	6%
Cannabis only	11%
All	6%

In summary, if three-quarters of the sample traded in either heroin or cocaine or both drugs, it seems equally important to note that almost two-thirds traded in one substance only. Of the poly-substance dealers, the bulk of these were buying and selling dance drugs. Finally, a small number (three) were associated with networks that traded in all illicit substances. We discuss the role of these middle market multi-commodity drug brokers later in the report, and we gathered further case studies describing these forms of multi-commodity drug brokerage in interviews with enforcement personnel.

Law enforcement interviews and other contacts

In addition to the prison interviews, interviews were conducted with law enforcement personnel by the two principle researchers. Contacts were selected from a list of 'key informants' that had been drawn up by the Home Office and consisted of individuals with appropriate experience from HMCE, NCS, NCIS, police forces and constabularies, and the Metropolitan Police.

In addition, and where it was felt to be appropriate, interviews were arranged with members of drug agencies who could provide alternative forms of local knowledge. Interviews were also arranged with a small number of lawyers with experience of trials involving drug offences. In all, 46 interviews were conducted with law enforcement personnel, plus three lawyers and eight drug agency personnel.

Table 1.5: *Interviews with enforcement personnel and others*

HMCE	13
NCIS	12
NCS	7
Police	14
Drug agencies	8
Lawyers	3
Total	57

The mechanism for arranging these interviews that worked best was if each law enforcement agency provided us with 'gatekeepers' who could alert individual officers that we would be contacting them, and give them the authority to be interviewed. Interviews with law enforcement personnel could touch upon some sensitive issues, such as the handling of informants and other intelligence matters, which would have been difficult without this prior authorisation. This was, of course, more difficult with individual police forces.

When contact was initially made by telephone, individuals were sent a brief one-page outline of the research and its aims prior to the interview. This included a summary of the areas that the interviews would touch upon, and also drew attention to the fact that one aim of these interviews was to generate case studies of middle market drug distribution networks. It was felt that, in addition to obtaining general insights into the middle market from law enforcement personnel, case studies would generate information that would be comparable to that obtained from prison interviews. Interviews with law enforcement personnel were not tape-recorded, unlike the prison interviews.

Officers were offered the option of preparing written case studies themselves, but most preferred to give verbal accounts, sometimes with reference to case notes and other records. Quite often it was necessary to arrange a second follow-up interview to obtain case studies following a preliminary 'ice-breaking' interview on more general themes. This meant that the conduct of law enforcement interviews was much more time consuming than had been anticipated at the outset.

By means of interviews with prisoners, law enforcement personnel and others, it was possible to generate approximately 70 case studies of middle market drug distribution networks, some of them very detailed. The body of this report is based on information collected in these ways, and in addition to field research material interspersed throughout the report, we have included in the form of an appendix a small number of brief case studies and vignettes on different themes, different levels of operation within drug markets, and networks dealing in different drug commodities.

2.   Defining the 'middle' market

There are no available definitions or consensus as to what constitutes the 'middle market' in terms of drug distribution. Typologies have been offered from USA research of various roles and functions involved in the distribution of both heroin and cocaine (Johnson *et al.*, 1985; Johnson *et al.*, 1992), although this research has predominantly focused on networks operating at or near retail or street level. A typology of varieties of upper-level drug dealers has also been constructed, based on cases prosecuted in New York City (Natarajan and Belanger, 1998). However, as acknowledged in one of these accounts, there is a tendency to provide 'a conceptual framework that is "too neat" to explain the very "messy reality"' of drug distribution (Johnson *et al.*, 1992: p. 71). A preliminary discussion will therefore be useful in terms of the how our own evidence points to conflicting definitions of the middle market.

Middle market drug distribution and organised crime

One immediate question that arises is the relationships between middle market drug distribution, however defined, and organised crime. There are considerable grounds for disagreement about the definition of 'organised crime' itself, both among criminologists and the personnel of different law enforcement agencies (Hagan, 1983; Maltz, 1976 & 1985; Albanese, 1996; Ruggiero, 1996: pp. 26-30). The dominant view, which is also in agreement with most popular images of organised crime, is of tightly organised, hierarchical forms of organisation. For some commentators, a crucial requirement for defining organised crime networks is the number of individuals involved, for others it is the time-span over which criminal activities take place.

Despite these differences, one common tendency is to view organised crime networks as extensive in their geographical reach within any given country, while also reaching beyond and across national boundaries. So, we find increasing mention of 'cross-border' crime or 'transnational', or even global, crime networks (Williams, 1993).

There is an obvious attraction in such views where drug trafficking is concerned. With the exception of synthetic drugs such as amphetamine or MDMA, illicit drug crops such as the opium poppy, coca plant and cannabis are harvested in distant parts of the globe and, by a variety of routes, processes and mechanisms, they are delivered to consumers in the most lucrative areas of drug demand, such as Europe and the USA. In this sense, drug markets are indelibly global and transnational in character (Woodiwiss, 1993).

Nevertheless, the view that we take here on the basis of the evidence gathered is that it is a mistake to see these organised crime networks as unified entities – monolithic and hierarchical. There are undoubtedly important aspects of transnational illicit markets that need to be better understood, as recently demonstrated by the USA economist Peter Reuter (Reuter, 2000). Even so, as Reuter himself argued in his study of upper level drug dealing in the USA, it is more useful to think of drug trafficking as partnerships between independent traders:

> The arrangements described were not so formal and permanent as either legitimate businesses or the traditional criminal organisations described... Most of the arrangements would be better described as small partnerships... Hierarchical organisations may exist, but they are not necessary for lucrative careers... Successful operation does not require creation of a large or enduring organisation... The trading relationships described by our informants were more like networks than like hierarchical organisations (Reuter and Haaga, 1989: pp. 40, 54).

This would accord with our view and the evidence collected in this research, both from interviews with imprisoned offenders and with law enforcement personnel. Hierarchies do sometimes exist, but they are by no means necessary, and individuals often occupy different positions within the system at different times. Most of the networks brought to our attention consist of a small number of individuals, freely trading with other groups of individuals. Nor was it uncommon to find dealers in the middle market who operate successfully alone. The number of customers who were supplied by a given network or individual was also correspondingly quite small, and people took the view that their own suppliers were only trading with a small number of customers like themselves – although this was often speculation, since drug dealers were typically poorly informed about the structure of networks above them in the supply chain.

In summary, there are two views about organised crime and drug markets. Customs and police operations working at the upper level of importation and wholesale dealing do sometimes reveal tightly-organised, hierarchical systems that endure over long periods of time. Sometimes, these are also linked by systems of kinship and ethnicity, such as those described by Ianni (1972) in his study of American, mafia-style crime networks, or Chin's (1990) study of Chinese gangs, secret societies and triads.

Equally, it is possible to work at the importation and wholesale level of the UK drugs market as part of much smaller, flexible trading partnerships. At lower levels of the middle market, similarly, one does sometimes find well-embedded criminal networks organised along the lines of the traditional 'family firm' (Hobbs, 2001a). However, this would appear to be increasingly less typical of the drugs middle market. Our evidence suggests that individuals can often find a niche within the middle market and establish themselves quite quickly, in terms of a secure network of suppliers and customers. This would not be possible within strictly hierarchical and centralised structures, which create what Arlacchi (1986: p. 195) in his study of the Mafia, describes as 'protective enclaves' to discourage the entry into the market of rivals and competitors. The most useful way to characterise serious crime networks operating within middle market drug distribution is as small, constantly mutating, flexible systems (Hobbs, 1997).

Where is the middle market?

If there are conflicting definitions of organised crime, we are not aware of any formal attempts at defining 'middle market' drug distribution. One aim of this research study was to attempt to clarify the meaning and scope of the middle market. This proves to be a highly complex question, where there is little consensus. In order to illustrate the nature of the difficulty, we will first provide some examples of how the term is used in different ways, both by law enforcement agencies and by those actively involved in drug markets.

A question invariably posed in interviews with law enforcement personnel was, 'What exactly do you mean by middle?'. Different views as to what and where the middle market was to be located were also expressed in these interviews. In interviews with Customs Officers, for example, it was common to encounter the response, 'I don't think I'll be able to help you, our sphere of operations is above the middle of the market'. Police drug squads, on the other hand, sometimes took the view that they worked below the level of the middle market. In which case, both these attitudes would imply that the middle market was to be located somewhere in-between customs and the police, presumably in the sphere currently occupied by the NCS.

In addition, in provincial drug squad interviews the notion of 'middle' was sometimes assumed to be one that mirrored force structures: 'Customs deal with importation, the NCS deal with the middle, we operate below'. Or, drug squad officers might take a different view on the lines that 'Customs and NCS deal with the high level, routine policing picks up arrests at the bottom, we're in the middle'.

In summary, there was very little consensus evident in the views expressed, which could even be quite opposed.

Describing the cocaine market, one police officer said: 'The middle, I suppose, that's the ounce dealers... That's what I'd call the middle market... We don't deal with that; drugs enforcement has gone up-stream in recent years'. (Source: NCIS)

In terms of heroin, I'd say it was the kilo dealers... the one and two kilo level people. That's my idea of the middle. (Source: NCIS)

Kilo dealers, in both heroin and cocaine, they're the middlemen. (Source: NCS)

In a global market, which is what drugs are, I'd say importation is the middle market. (Source: NCIS)

It's all middle. (Source: Metropolitan Police)

In prison interviews, individuals also used the notion of 'middle' in different ways. Someone might see himself 'in the middle' in terms of handling the transport route between, for example, Dutch warehouses and domestic buyers. Or, in between importation and whatever went on below.

We didn't import, we bought it off importers and sold it on... we were in the middle. (Male, age 34 years. Source: prison interview)

In prison interviews, people quite often described themselves as being in the 'middle'. Interestingly, however, the term was employed irrespective of the level at which they operated in the market.

A young man who worked as a bit-part player, one of a team of dealers in a form of employee role, said of his relationship to his employer: 'On the street, I'd say I was quite high. If someone said, can you get so-and-so, pills whatever, I'd get them off X [his boss]. But in terms of the actual business, where they came from, the money side, he was higher up than me. I'd say he was in the middle, he was the middleman.' (Male, age 19 years. Source: prison interview)

A European foreign national, based in Holland, was close to pill-manufacturers of ecstasy tablets and could obtain high quality cocaine, although he was less interested in cocaine since it was less profitable. He had half-a-dozen customers, including a group from the North of England who would buy from him and import into the UK loads of 30,000 pills and a couple of kilos of cocaine. 'The man above me, he was close to the pill-maker. He was buying 600,000 every three or four days. I just used to purchase on demand… You want it, I can get it. I was more or less a middleman.' (Male, age 42 years. Source: prison interview)

A young woman operated a single-handed operation around the club scene, selling 1,000 ecstasy tablets and a quarter to half a kilogram of amphetamine per week. She described her function in the market as a service to others: 'It's just friends, and friends of friends really. I'd buy the drugs I knew they would want – Es, whizz, a bit of coke, weed, what have you – people would phone in their orders for themselves and their friends, and I'd deliver before the weekend. It was simple as that. I was doing them a service… I was the go-between.' (Female, age 21 years. Source: prison interview)

Two young men worked as a team, buying kilo loads of cocaine and selling it in ounce and multi-ounce deals of cocaine and crack-cocaine. 'It was a business like any other. We knew where we could get hold of cocaine at a decent price, and we knew people who wanted to buy it. We were in the middle.' (Male, age 29 years. Source: prison interview)

The role of middlemen is often understood in terms of risk management and security. For example, traffickers who organise transactions but who do not handle drugs themselves employ expendable intermediaries as 'cut outs' who collect and deliver drug loads on their behalf, and who might even be unaware of the identity of their employer or other people in the network (Dorn *et al.*, 1998). Some of our prison interviews were with people who claimed to have been in this position, especially the small number who had been recruited as 'mules':

I was the mug. I didn't even know what I was carrying… I'd just been and had a nice holiday in the Caribbean, all expenses paid… Now I'm sitting here. Like I said, I was the mug. (Male, age 28 years. Source: prison interview)

I didn't know who I was dealing with. I just had to deliver the suitcase to a hotel when I got off the plane and someone would meet me there. (Female, age 34 years. Source: prison interview)

In another interview with a young man who was a 'runner' for a middle market drug broker, he explained how his boss kept him in the dark and explained that it was for his own benefit:

He said it was for my own good, like. He said you're not going to know these other people so if anything goes wrong you can only grass up yourself, and like if they grass anybody up they don't know who I am, so it's better that way. (Male, age 20 years. Source: prison interview)

The function of middlemen and intermediaries, however, was more commonly described in business terms:

A man who arranged cannabis and ecstasy importations from Holland on behalf of other people described the operation in the following terms: 'There was three parties involved: the man who was actually prepared to bring it through the docks, the driver, then we had the guy who was actually purchasing it, the recipient, and me in the middle. My being the middle man, obviously I didn't want the two parties to meet, because once they met that left me nowhere... Of course I never met the actual buyer. I always met someone else on his behalf, another middleman if you like.' (Male, age 55 years. Source: prison interview)

Someone who bought multiple ounces of cocaine and heroin each week and supplied to others saw the function of intermediaries and middlemen in drug markets as much in terms of business and money-making as security:'A lot of people can be very secretive and most people will only know the person above them, and they don't normally know who that person is getting their stuff from... They could by-pass them... If somebody else can skip past them on the ladder and get them cheaper, you know, then they are out of business... Yes I suppose there's a lot of secrecy.' (Male, age 30 years. Source: prison interview)

Making sense of differing perceptions of the middle market

Different permutations of these kinds of responses point to the inherently problematic notion of the middle market. We can point to three broadly defined ways of defining the 'middle'.

- If the drugs business is understood as a truly global market, then one might say that the 'middle' is the *point of importation.*

- On the other hand, from the perspective of someone higher up the chain, it consists of those networks *that join up systems of cultivation and production* – where laboratories and other production systems are located back in source countries –

with systems of global distribution, for example, where heroin is being routed to North America or Europe, via Balkan or African routes, etc.

- In a rather more parochial view, in terms of domestic systems of supply and demand, 'the middle' is *something that happens between importation and retail supply to consumers.*

It is this third sphere of activity that provides the focus of our study, although it is necessary to enter one further element of complexity. Drug distribution networks are continually mutating and much of this traditional middle ground – between importers and retailers – is increasingly now played out in mainland Europe. Middle market drug brokers, regionally-based and operating in the UK, liaise with systems of drug brokerage and warehousing in the Netherlands and elsewhere, and are directly involved in importation. This further complicates the 'middle market'.

Each of the definitions of the 'middle' as set out above is equally valid. To an important extent, what is meant by 'middle' depends upon the individual agent's point of view. That is, what looks like 'middle' to one actor will look like 'upper' or 'lower' to another. This refers to both enforcement personnel and to offenders.

All participants (enforcers and offenders) are only partially sighted. We noted that customs officers, when asked what happens below a certain level of transaction, would often say 'we're un-sighted'. NCS officers would only understand a drug smuggling and distribution network up to a certain point, but not beyond. In both cases, whether 'above' or 'below', it becomes a matter of guesswork and inference. Similarly, offenders frequently only understood limited aspects of the drug business network of which they were a part.

Drug markets, and perceptions of drug markets are highly fragmented. We return to this in our conclusions. In terms of the methodology that we adopted, early in the research process it became clear that the most successful strategy would be one that attempted to provide viewpoints and case studies from as many different positions in drug markets as possible. There is no one place called the 'middle'. The perspective of retail level heroin dealers – looking upwards into a supply hierarchy of which they have only a dim outline – proved as useful and valid as the views of upper level dealers looking downwards into the murky depths of the low-level retail trade. In one sense, located as each individual and network is between someone who wants to sell and someone who wants to buy, they are all 'in the middle'.

3.

The organisation and price structure of UK drug markets

It will first be useful to sketch out the structure of the markets for different commodities that provides the economic environment in which drug traffickers operate. Where an indication of prices is offered, these involve information gathered in field research, rather than published data such as that provided by HMCE or NCIS. In a short-term project such as ours, this means that the collation of price information is subject to regional variations and market anomalies such as how closely supplier and purchaser are connected. In terms of prison interviews, where offenders were arrested some time ago, price indications might also involve fluctuations across time. As a result, price data are not always comparable. A key finding, however, is that fluctuations in prices at importation and wholesale levels do not appear to translate into street prices.

The price data presented in this report have been compared with the information on drug prices collated by NCIS, which apart from some very fragmentary evidence on retail level prices (NCIS, 2000: p. 17) is not in the public domain. The two sets of data are strictly non-comparable since NCIS data reflect the wide range of prices reported by different police forces. Nevertheless, our price information falls comfortably within this range, tending towards the lower end of the spectrum.

Heroin

Intelligence sources agree that 80 to 90 per cent of heroin entering the UK is under Turkish control. This control is exercised by extended family connections with a base in London, but with a 'line of command' extending back to different regions of Turkey. Formerly, South Asian (i.e. Pakistani and Indian) networks were dominant at importation level, but during the 1990s have ceded to Turkish-controlled shipment routes and are now often content to occupy a middle market brokerage role within the UK. It is many years since South East Asian connections to the 'Golden Triangle' of Burma, Laos and Thailand have been observable as a significant importation route.

Even so, occasional anomalies are found within this pattern, such as the shipment of a few large loads of heroin originating in Pakistan via Kenya. Intelligence operations are inevitably focused on one particular system of transportation, and while they might yield high quality information on those systems, intelligence gathering can become a self-fulfilling prophecy that is 'blind' to alternative shipment systems, which are peripheral to the field of vision. This is why we recommend that systematic methods of chemical 'fingerprinting' should be developed at all levels of the heroin market, whereby testing at the middle and lower levels of the market might indicate blind-spots in high-level intelligence.

In terms of prices, heroin originating in Afghanistan (but largely controlled by ethnic Turks in the UK) is transported in bulk loads and can be obtained by transporters/importers for as little as £600 per kilo. If a shipment of, for example, 100 kilos becomes available it will be traded amongst importers and wholesalers at £6,000 to £8,000 per kilo in transactions of 20, 30 or 40 kilos. Various systems of brokerage and intermediaries, sometimes but not always involving Turks, connect this wholesale level of trade with middle-level brokers at a price between £17,000 for a multi-kilo purchase or £22,000 for a single kilo load. At this level it will often be bulked out with cutting agents before being sold in ounces at £800 to £1,000 (equivalent to £28,000 to £35,000 per kilo) to retail level dealers or middle market intermediaries who regularly buy in units of a quarter kilo of 'nine-bar'. However, there is no systematic knowledge of at what level in the market heroin is diluted; our field observations indicate that some middle market drug brokers buying in five kilo batches will add 'bash' (caffeine, paracetamol or other bulking agents) but whether this also happens at higher levels is not clear.

An alternative system of heroin importation co-exists with this dominant bulk-load Turkish structure, involving South Asian families and networks. Heroin purchased in Pakistan for £2,000 per kilo is transported by air courier in 10 to 15 kilo loads. There would be costs in terms of bribes to officials in Pakistan, and, in some forms of operation, in payments to corrupt baggage handlers at UK airports who facilitate transit. This was generally poor quality heroin, which was distributed to a number of regionally-based dealers who bought one to two kilo amounts at a price of £14,000 to £16,000 per kilo. Selling in ounces, these regionally-based brokers could easily double their money.

Cocaine

The structure of the cocaine market is less clear from our observations, and our impression is that this is both because it is more complex and less settled than the distribution system for heroin. It is also likely that intelligence and enforcement agencies have a less complete understanding. As a consequence, the price structure of the cocaine market seems to be less well charted than that of other drugs, and is possibly more volatile.

In terms of bulk shipments, Colombian networks, based in London, appear to perform much the same controlling role as Turks in relation to heroin. However, there are overlaps between cocaine importation systems and those for synthetics, with Dutch and Belgian warehousing operations playing a crucial role and trading directly with UK national middle market brokers.

In terms of prices, in Colombia the price of cocaine is roughly £2,000 per kilo. In the UK, Colombians are said to sell multi-kilo loads at about £19,000 to £22,000 per kilo, but with prices ranging up to £30,000 at this level[1]. Alternatively, cocaine can be purchased and collected by middle-level dealers from Dutch-based middlemen for lower prices of £16,000 to £17,000 per kilo, but with the added risks of importation and transportation costs.

Through a variety of systems of brokerage and intermediaries, cocaine is distributed to local/regional drug brokers who typically buy a few kilos every fortnight, and sell to several kinds of customers. A typical operation would involve a middle market dealer trading one kilo per week, buying at £20,000 to £25,000 per kilo or £7,500 per nine-bar unit (quarter-kilo). This would be sold in ounce or multi-ounce units at £1,000 plus per ounce (equivalent to £35,000 plus per kilo), although 'washed up' and sold in crack form this could yield a return as high as £4,000 to £5,000 per ounce (equivalent to £141,000 to £176,000 per kilo). Alternatively, at a lower level an individual might be prepared to pay £8,000 for nine ounces of good quality cocaine (equivalent to £31,000 per kilo) on a regular basis, which is sold for £1,200 per ounce (a mark-up of 35%), either direct to consumers or to retail dealers selling on in grams. People buying in smaller quantities such as this might also buy a 'half bar' (125 grams) for £4,000 and sell in ounce units in the same way.

A simpler kind of cocaine market structure involves importation from the Caribbean in smaller loads employing couriers, either as 'stuffers' and 'swallowers' or carrying cocaine in luggage. In a typical case, a small London-based Jamaican team could access cocaine in the Caribbean for £12,000 per kilo, which was brought over in 15 kilos loads. On arrival in London, the cocaine was immediately 'washed up' and sold in its crack form for £18,000 to £20,000 to a middle market broker supplying a network of retail outlets.

Heroin and cocaine: summary

The distribution systems for heroin and cocaine thus appear to mirror each other, with two co-existing systems: one involving bulk shipments to wholesalers, and the other involving 'small-but-often' loads carried by couriers.

---

1   Shortages on the European mainland caused a sharp upward fluctuation in January 2000, before levelling down again. As a consequence, some of the data collected are non-comparable since prison interviews would have covered periods prior to this recent price rise.

The cocaine market is seen as less profitable than that for heroin, at least for those operating below importation, something remarked upon by offenders who had traded in both drugs. Price fluctuations in the cocaine market are also noted at kilo level transactions in the Netherlands. Our impression is that the price information that we have collected for cocaine might be somewhat unreliable, in that it might not allow for sufficient profit margins for middle market dealers, although one form of business model used by dealers in the middle market is to operate on the principle of a high turnover that compensates for a small unit profit. The use of adulterants could also enlarge profits to mid-tier brokers. The position in the markets at which adulterants are used is unclear for both heroin and cocaine, which could significantly alter profit margins in the middle market.

However, cocaine middle market dealers who sell at ounce and multi-ounce levels reported that they did not use cutting agents because customers demand a quality product. This is an important difference that distinguishes between middle market practices in the heroin and cocaine markets. It is possibly a consequence of the fact that in the cocaine powder (hydrochloride) market the end-point consumer is more discerning than the end-point heroin user. Profits would appear to be considerably enlarged, however, when middle market traders 'wash up' cocaine themselves and sell the product in its crack form.

Ecstasy

The market for ecstasy and related pills works strictly on a quantity discount basis. Ecstasy pills can be bought for a unit cost of 0.50p direct from a Dutch-based laboratory or pill-maker in loads of 100,000 or 200,000 for importation, and there will be a mark up as these are sold in smaller loads of 10,000 to 20,000 pills. Alternatively, a Dutch-based middleman will supply UK nationals with loads of 10,000 to 30,000 tablets at a unit price of £1.00 that have been bought direct from the manufacturer at 0.50p. A lower-level UK dealer will be able to purchase at a unit cost of £2.50 to £3 when buying a couple of thousand per week. These will be sold by this mid-to-low level dealer at £5 per pill to people buying in units of hundreds who are typically retail level dealers supplying networks of friends. The cost to the consumer varies, according to quality and how well acquainted retailer and end-point consumer are, but could be as little as £7.50 or as much as £10 to £15 when purchased in clubs. Customer loyalty to brand-name pills, identified by logos such as Superman, Mitsubishi, Tweety Pie, etc. seems to be largely unfounded since modern pill machines can produce any number of different logos from the same batch of powder. Customer loyalty to individual dealers with a reputation for quality sales is better founded.

Amphetamine

Amphetamine is either imported from mainland Europe, or produced in domestic laboratories. The scale varies from small-scale labs with a capacity to produce 10 to 15 kilo batches, to large ones producing 100 kilo loads on a repeat basis. The smaller type of producer connects directly with the middle-level market selling five kilo loads packed in the form of half-kilo 'balls' at 80 to 85 per cent purity. It is sometimes believed that 'base' amphetamine is cut once by these purchasers to yield street-level purity of four to five per cent, although case study evidence points to different practices.

In one scenario, an intermediary believed to be quite close to a small-scale domestic manufacturer was buying amphetamine at £1,900 to £2,100 per kilo, although usually in fractions of a kilo. This was sold as high purity amphetamine 'base' to close contacts for £200 per ounce (equivalent to £7,000 per kilo), a highly profitable exchange, and sometimes slightly less. One of these contacts sold the product without adding adulterants at £15 to £20 per gram, again a profitable exchange on outlay.

In a different form of transaction, nine ounces of amphetamine could reportedly be purchased for £450, which means either that the purchaser was close to the manufacturing source or that the product had been considerably adulterated. This would then be further adulterated by a factor of two, and sold in ounces at £200 to £250 unit cost. At consumer level, 'wraps' of 'speed' or 'whizz' are sold at £8 to £10 each, containing approximately 0.1 grams of amphetamine in a one-to-ten mix. The 'bulking-out' of amphetamine with adulterants clearly has a major impact on the price structure, meaning that prices between different levels of the market are non-comparable.

It is important to note that the amphetamine market is segmented. In the 'base' market, high purity amphetamine is sold on at different levels with little or no 'bulking out of the product, even at retail and consumer level. This is quite distinguishable from the 'speed' or 'whizz' market where cutting agents are added at each level, and the end-product is low purity.

Cannabis

We have not collected a great deal of evidence on cannabis importation, warehousing and wholesale transactions, whether in terms of transportation routes or prices. One operation, which was described as typical, involved the regular purchase of 70 to 100 kilo loads at approximately £1,250 to £1,500 per kilo, the price depending on quality and whether the consignment was a cash purchase or on credit. This was sold in five to ten kilo loads to a network of middle market brokers, with a price mark-up of £25 to £50 per kilo. This network involved high volume turnover, of 70 to 100 kilos each week.

At the level of multi-kilo sales, the price fell quite sharply a few years ago. Whereas it stood at roughly £2,000 per kilo, it is now possible to buy at £1,200 or £1,300 per kilo. However the retail price has remained remarkably stable at £15 for one-eighth of an ounce (3.5 grams) for many years, although there are quantity discounts for end-point consumers.

The market for cannabis has been complicated by the importation of Dutch 'skunk', and also by increasing domestic production in the UK. Relatively modest scale cannabis growers, with a growing and harvesting cycle of ten weeks, might produce three kilos every three months, which can be sold at £4,000 to £4,500 per kilo – considerably higher than cannabis resin prices. The main overhead costs for this type of operation are rent and electricity, with one estimate that half a gram of herbal cannabis could be produced per watt of lighting equipment capacity. We have collected no evidence on much more substantial cannabis farming enterprises in the UK.

Conclusions

The economic structure of drug trafficking that has been sketched out above is complex and constantly mutating. Even so, it is somewhat surprising how few links in the supply chain there are between importation and retail level (cf. Reuter and Haaga, 1989: p. 46). In the case of heroin, for example, this can be as few as four levels: from 100 kilo upwards bulk shipments at importation; through 20 to 40 kilo wholesale dealers; to one to ten kilo middle-level drug brokers; to retail level dealers buying in ounces and selling in grams and £20 'bags'.

Within this sometimes elusive price structure, different commodities behave in different ways. The 'street price' of ecstasy would appear to have fallen in the early 1990s and then increased again, for example, whereas the retail cost of cocaine has tended to fall. In terms of street price, both heroin and cannabis have remained remarkably stable for many years, in spite of a sharp fall in the kilo price of cannabis a few years ago, and record opium crop yields reported from Afghanistan. Our data do nevertheless indicate that the street price of heroin has within the past 12 to 18 months fallen quite sharply in some areas to as low as £35 to £40 per gram, although this is by no means a consistent trend and we have no information on purity levels.

It would seem that it is not supply-demand pressures that cause price fluctuations or price stability in drug markets, at least at street level. We have already noted the sudden surge in the wholesale price of cocaine in the late months of 1999 that did not result in any price fluctuations lower in the market. Importers and bulk wholesalers were either prepared to take a reduction in profits in order to maintain customer loyalty (which would suggest a relative scarcity of supply), or to bulk out their product with adulterants to restore profit margins. However, customer preference in the cocaine market for a high quality product militates against this.

The insensitivity of street prices to fluctuations in crop yields, importation price levels or wholesale availability implies that street prices are not a reliable indicator of the success or failure of upper-level interception efforts. In the USA, where the price series data for cocaine are much more sophisticated (Caulkins, 1994), there are some indications that interdiction efforts can have short term effects in depressing street prices (Crane et al., 1997), although this remains a matter of controversy. The much more limited price information that we have collected in what is essentially a research study employing qualitative research methods suggests that whereas illicit drug prices across the board are either stable or falling, participation in middle market drug distribution remains highly profitable.

One final note on the economic environment is that in the UK we do not possess systematic data on purity at different levels in the market. Purity testing is not routinely carried out on drugs seized, since it is often not of relevance in making a case for prosecution. Systematic purity-testing at all levels of the drug market is an imperative intelligence requirement if one is to understand more completely the economic workings and vulnerabilities of drug brokerage in the 'middle market' and elsewhere.

4. The internal organisation of drug dealing networks

The previous chapter dealt with the external environment with which drug dealing criminal networks must contend. This chapter examines some important aspects of the internal structure of these networks. A principal concern is how trust and order are maintained in an illicit market where contracts cannot be legally upheld. This includes a discussion in the following chapter of the role of violence in drug dealing networks. We also examine ways in which these networks vary in terms of whether they trade in multi-commodities or single commodities, and in this context we introduce the concept of the middle-level multi-commodity drug broker who is a vital linkage point in the middle market, and whose role will be further discussed in chapter 6.

Family and ethnicity

Ties between members of criminal networks involving kinship and ethnicity have traditionally been essential means of maintaining trust and order. These remain important, although not so exclusively as previously. Family and kinship ties are often most prominent at higher levels of drug trafficking, as for example, in the dominant Turkish control of the transportation of bulk heroin supplies, its warehousing in mainland Europe, and importation into the UK. In the cocaine market similar roles are occupied by London-based Colombians. South Asian networks, on the other hand, are found at lower levels of the domestic heroin market in many regions, having been displaced at importation levels by increased Turkish involvement in the 1990s.

Ethnically bonded networks such as these involve people whose family origins are in drug-producing countries and regions, and these regional affiliations are often exploited commercially in terms of importation. Otherwise, at a more local level, their methods of working closely resemble the traditional 'family firm' networks that remain important in many British towns and cities. Those involved in drug dealing and other forms of criminal enterprise typically comprise small, tightly bonded groups of individuals with relationships going back a long way – whether in terms of kinship, coming from the same neighbourhood, or growing up at school together.

Networks based on familial, ethnic and neighbourhood relationships have often been described in the wider research literature on 'organised crime'. Distinct localities and kinship connections were as much in evidence in London's fabled East End 'underworld', as in the race-course and gambling 'mobs' of the inter-war years in Sheffield and elsewhere, or the so-called 'razor gangs' of Glasgow, which were also interlaced with sectarian religious conflicts (Bean, 1981; Samuel, 1981; Hobbs, 1988; Davies, 1998). Embedded ties of these kinds – based on kinship, territory and other 'non-negotiable' qualities – constitute trust variables that guarantee a commitment beyond self-interest (Gambetta, 1988). 'If a group all speaks the same language, has the same village roots, possesses the same myths and cultural norms, then it can function as a unit with greater trust and understanding' (Lupsha, 1981: p. 34; and see Reuter, 1983: p. 115 and Hobbs, 2001b).

Relationships such as these produce hybrid forms of organisation between business association and friendship:

> A white British drug dealer set up a middle market operation trading in multiple kilos of cocaine. The network of which he was part stretched across the country and involved one of the UK's most prominent crime families. However the dealer relied heavily upon a friendship group going back to primary school to staff his part of the operation, and personnel were paid mainly in drugs and free holidays. (Source: Police)

> A black British man of African-Caribbean descent operated a middle market heroin distribution network dealing in five kilos per week at the height of his operation. The network embraced four cities – London, Southampton, Bristol and Manchester – these locations being determined solely by the fact that close friends and members of his extended family had settled in these places. (Source: prison interview)

These embedded ties can offer more flexibility than purely business associations, since they are firmly rooted in implicit understandings, loyalty and trust which extend far beyond the purely functional concerns of 'price and delivery' that typify arm's length business relationships. Even so, their benefits can be paradoxical and imply limitations as well as advantages (Uzzi, 1997). If a drug dealing network is to flourish and expand within the current drug market, self-imposed boundaries of kinship and ethnicity impose barriers that must be overcome. Too much reliance on these more traditional forms of trust relation can become a liability, since an exclusive dependence on embedded ties can trap the firm in a closed network that would inevitably choke itself. Consequently, flexibility that combines embedded ties with more conventionally business-like arm's length relationships is emerging as a more common form of association.

A Turkish middle market network strongly based on embedded family ties was involved in the importation, wholesale storage and domestic distribution of substantial quantities of heroin. The Turkish network relied upon Dutch people to warehouse the drugs in Holland and Belgium, however, and at different times employed both Dutch and South Asian (Pakistani) drivers to transport heroin into the UK. (Source: HMCE)

Turkish wholesalers must also maintain effective contacts with UK nationals and others who are their customers and who buy one to five kilo, or five to ten kilo loads within the national and regional distribution systems. Nevertheless, the crossing of these ethnic boundaries is potentially a point of vulnerability and Turkish heroin wholesalers will often employ Turkish middlemen for the purpose of dealing with lower-level purchasers. A different form of ethnic cross-over involves tightly-knit Pakistani distribution networks that were developed in the North of England during the period when South Asians dominated heroin importation. These have now adapted to Turkish control of global transport systems, proving their versatility by buying from Turks while still controlling a lower tier of the middle market.

Finally, in an inner London Bengali community where heroin misuse has become a major issue, a well-placed informant indicated that some years ago it was necessary to do business with Turkish dealers further up the supply chain, but that now it was more fluid. Bengali networks were arranging importation on their own behalf, white middle market brokers had become involved, and Nigerian suppliers were also said to be in a strong position. (Source: Metropolitan Police; NCS; field interview)

It is most important in this context that the middle market is not portrayed purely as the domain of non-white minority ethnic groups. One the contrary, we have ample evidence of white indigenous groups who also trade and collaborate across ethnic boundaries, often with embedded ties at their core.

A cluster of white, locally-embedded networks linked by 'gofers' arranged for the importation of 30 kilograms of cocaine from Belgium using two couriers. The cocaine was believed to be controlled by Colombians, working through Spanish and Italian intermediaries. Such an operation required networked collaboration involving a range of both embedded and arm's length relationships across local, regional, international and linguistic boundaries. (Source: NCIS)

A white family firm has been buying heroin from the London-based Turkish community for many years and regularly visited the Turkish families' homes in northern Cyprus.

The younger members of the local firm have now established their own drug importation business and have established a base in Holland through which they are able, through their London-based Turkish associates, to facilitate importation into the UK. They have utilised connections in the haulage trade as well as using foot passengers aboard ferries and driving private motor vehicles to enter the UK. (Source: NCIS)

Imprisonment as a facilitator of crime networks

Imprisonment is also a key generator of networks that has major implications for cross-regional collaboration, as offenders from different locales mix with each other while serving prison sentences (Shover, 1996: pp. 162-74; Barnes *et al.*, 2000: p. 41; Reuter and Haaga, 1989: p. 38). The shared experiences of imprisonment can cut across forms of inter-regional mistrust and hostility that otherwise would act as obstacles to cross-regional co-operation. Many of our interviewees indicated that prison was an extremely important generator of information and contacts for the drugs trade, and that serious crime networks that include and overlap with the middle market feature associations that are either forged in prison or facilitated via secondary relationships. Often it appeared that the experience of imprisonment assisted individuals in locating opportunities that had already been identified by established networks, and that within the prison system, notable well-established 'brands' were especially influential (Hobbs, 2001a).

A violent burglar, with just one conviction, who was released from prison in the 1980s, was introduced to the possibilities of the drug trade by established Liverpool drug dealers whom he met while in prison. Based initially on connections provided by his prison mentors, this man rose during the 1990s to become a major dealer in a range of drugs and also utilised prison connections to recruit employees, notably drivers. (Source: NCS)

A young man from a small town in Wales was imprisoned in the early 1990s on a charge of possession with intent to supply ecstasy. In prison, he struck up a friendship with two men who were using heroin, developed a heroin habit himself, and began dealing in prison. Alerted to the profitability of heroin, and with the need to fund his habit upon his release from prison, his prison friends facilitated his contact with an associate in the East Midlands who 'sorted him out' with supplies of heroin which were initially on credit. From this start, he built up a heroin distribution network around his hometown in Wales, selling ounces and multi-ounce deals to six or seven customers who were closer to the retail trade. He continued to buy his heroin from his contact in the geographically-remote East Midlands, as someone regarded as reliable and loyal to him in his time of need. (Source: prison interview)

A man in his early 30s from north east Scotland served a five year prison term for violence, during which he developed a heroin habit. On release, he established a drugs business that involved sending a runner to buy half a kilo of heroin four or five times a week from suppliers in Manchester. He did not know who his suppliers were, or what kind of network they operated: 'No, not interested... It's none of your business, better not to know'. He had made contact with them through his prison sentence, 'I knew them from the jail... Got a few telephone numbers from people that knew them... just wrote down people's numbers I knew would be able to help me out when the time came.' (Source: prison interview)

Mr. H. was a professional man in the East Midlands with a heroin habit and also sold quantities of cocaine to his local friendship network that he obtained from close friends in London. When his heroin supplier was imprisoned, he gave Mr. H. an introduction to his own suppliers based in Merseyside, with a 'reference' as a reliable man who could handle the amounts which he had been dealing. His drugs business prospered from thereon, buying and selling a 'nine-bar' of cocaine each week, a quarter to a half kilo of heroin, and several hundred ecstasy tablets. (Source: prison interview)

'Clubbing' as a system of fraternity

If the notion of the prison as a 'university of crime' has a long historical pedigree, it might also be useful to think of the clubbing scene as a modern system of fraternity that can facilitate drug networks and highly accelerated drug dealing careers. As already indicated, the supply of drugs around the clubbing scene (and not necessarily in clubs themselves) typically involves the cluster of 'dance drugs': ecstasy, amphetamine, and also sometimes cocaine powder. Through prison interviews we have collected a number of case studies of individuals who rose rapidly in this context to become serious middle market drugs brokers. With no prior experience of drug dealing, within the space of a few months, an individual could establish him or herself as the supplier to a network of retailers and club dealers, selling anything from 1,000 to 3,000 ecstasy tablets per week, half a kilo of amphetamine, a few ounces of cocaine, and maybe a few kilos of cannabis, yielding a profit of several thousand pounds per week. In spite of the scale of this drug dealing business, the extent to which buyers are regarded as 'friends' or 'customers' is typically blurred within these transactions (Ward and Pearson, 1997). In prison interviews, there was an uncanny similarity in the way in which drug dealers described their rapid rise within this fraternity of regular club-goers:

> It kind of escalates quite easily... especially on the clubbing scene... it gets around that you can sort people out for drugs, and friends of friends... that sort of thing. (Male, age 30 years. Source: prison interview)

> Once I started, other people got to hear and that type of thing, and it escalates very quickly. I mean in the end, we're talking about like 1,000 tablets a week and like nine ounces of amphetamine... you find more people coming back saying, you know, instead of the tenner we're having £25 worth, so it goes up like that, it grows very quickly... I was on the club scene every week, meeting different people, socialising, people come saying can you get me some... And as soon as it started, phew, it got out of control really. (Female, age 21 years. Source: prison interview)

> I don't know, it's just friends that know friends isn't it? You know, I could say I've sold to over like three hundred people, but they may go and sell it over to somebody else... I didn't run it like a business, not really, it's just a friend of mine knows someone, he says, "He can sort you out", and it goes from there. (Male, age 21 years. Source: prison interview)

> It just went on from there. You know, then their friends want, and their friends want and then it's just escalated... Yes I was selling two-and-half thousand pills in a weekend, four kilos of weed, LSD, speed, four ounces of coke... Their friends want, and friends want, and friends want, and eventually you've got other people who want to start dealing and then dealers buy from you, and it's a sky rocket before you even know it... I don't agree with selling in clubs, it's more like pushing drugs. I didn't push drugs. I didn't push drugs at all. I did a social thing for friends, and then it just got bigger. (Male, age 30 years. Source: prison interview)

Size and division of labour

Drug trafficking networks undoubtedly differ in size and complexity. At lower levels in the market, the tendency is for these networks to be quite small and not uncommonly single-handed. A well-organised individual can, for example, sell 2,000 to 3,000 ecstasy tablets per week, plus a few ounces of cocaine and a couple kilos of cannabis. Perhaps it is more usual, however, to work in teams where one person has the connections, holds the purse strings and arranges purchases and cash transactions, with one or more junior partners acting as 'runners' collecting and delivering packages.

In terms of the bulk shipment and importation of heroin and cocaine, intelligence sources depict complex hydra-like networks stretching across national boundaries, often involving close ethnic and kinship links, and with a division of labour that compartmentalises the responsibility for drug purchases, transportation arrangements, warehousing, drug sales and customer relations, and cash handling. Even so, the core membership of such networks will tend to comprise no more than four or five people. Moreover, supply chains tend to be short as Reuter and Haaga (1989: p. 46) also note in their USA study.

In general, it seems that, at all levels, successful drug trafficking networks are relatively small in terms of core members. Although there might be a wider fringe of bit-part players and wage labourers who perform small but essential parts of the operation: 'baby-sitting' a bulk purchase of heroin for a wholesaler; bagging up quantities of drugs for retail sale; purchasing the glassware for an illicit laboratory; testing the purity of heroin for a middle-level broker; etc.

Cash transactions and credit cascades

Some earlier research, particularly in the USA, has characterised drug markets as a system of rolling credit fronts, whereby drugs are supplied without the requirement of cash up-front, and payment comes back from the purchaser at a later point when the drugs (or a proportion of them) have been sold.

There appear to be no hard-and-fast rules in the UK drug economy. Supplies will certainly sometimes be 'laid on' to a trusted customer, either cash free or at a substantial discount, with the requirement to complete payment at a later point. However, other suppliers always seem to require cash up front. It depends so often on the circumstances, or the precise nature of the operation.

For example, where a drug broker uses a 'runner' to deliver drugs to customers, often the runner will either not be trusted to handle cash or simply not required to. The runner might not even know whether the cash has been paid up-front for any particular delivery, or whether it will come back to his employer at a different time and by a different route. Some brokers employ people specifically to collect cash, and these people might never handle drugs at all. A different arrangement is one whereby the broker uses his employee to drum up business, with the requirement that customers so recruited must hand the cash over to the runner who delivers this to the broker in return for the required quantity of drugs. At the other extreme, some drug business relationships systematically operate as a form of credit cascade, whereby the cash travels back up the line of supply on an agreed timescale in order to finance a further cycle of drug importation and distribution.

Separating drug transactions and cash transactions is not simply a question of trust. In terms of security, it does not make sense to have the drugs and cash in the same place at any one time. Since, in the event of arrest, then both drugs and cash are lost. Jacobs (2000) has also recently conducted a research study highlighting the high incidence of robberies within drug markets and the fact that drug dealers are extremely lucrative targets for robbery.

Single-commodity and multi-commodity markets and dealers

This is an important distinction, and one of the most important indications from this preliminary research is that multi-commodity drug brokers – who sit between wholesalers and retailers – can occupy a crucial position in the 'middle market'.

In the first chapter, we indicated a typology of mono- and multi-commodity drug dealing, whereby drug markets are segmented and different middle market dealers trade in different combinations of drugs. In some cases this is a market-led decision. For example, middle-level dealers supplying people around the clubbing scene will tend to trade in those drugs – amphetamine, ecstasy, and sometimes cocaine – that are most in demand in that setting. At other times, the choice might be determined by availability. More than one middle market dealer complained that cocaine could be sometimes difficult to access at the right price. Or, in the case of heroin, there are middle market dealers who adopt a moral stance, and although they are prepared to trade in most other drugs they will not get involved with heroin.

> Mr. B. who was the head of a well-established family firm had been involved in drugs and crime throughout his life, working mainly in transportation and warehousing where drugs were concerned. He had also been involved in trading counterfeit money, forged motor vehicle certificates, and other types of fraud. In the drugs trade he acted as a distributor and supplier to other middle market dealers, often people that he had met in prison. He has been involved in amphetamine,

ecstasy, cannabis (both skunk and resin) and cocaine – but never heroin. Neither he nor his customers are interested in heroin. Heroin is regarded as a dirty business, and the objections of this man and others like him remain essentially moral. (Source: HMCE)

A young man who operated in the middle market, supplying to dealers around the club scene, traded in substantial quantities of amphetamine, ecstasy, cannabis, LSD and cocaine. But there were some drugs that he would not involve himself with. 'I don't think, you know, I'm not a bad person inside. I'm not like a drug pusher... I wouldn't deal in crack, and I wouldn't deal in heroin because those are dirty drugs. They're scum drugs... You don't see people who are ravers going out and mugging people so they can get a pill for the weekend, you know... It's a clean drug, well I think so. And you see people doing crack, heroin, mugging people just so they can get drugs... I disagree with crack and heroin.' (Male, age 30 years. Source: prison interview)

For others, their decision to deal in a limited range of drugs is determined by the perceived risks and penalties. One experienced, high-level cannabis dealer described his view of the segmented market in the following terms:

There are plenty of people out there who deal in everything. When there's no dope [cannabis] about they'll turn over charley [cocaine], when there's no charley about they'll do speed, or run three or four different things together. The smack dealers tend to run on their own. They might do smack and charley, but I've never found a bloke dealing dope and smack. It doesn't happen. They're totally separate businesses, because it's a totally different game... They might go to a guy who's connected with the charley business, but they certainly don't want to go to a guy who's connected to smack because if it comes on top, then big problem, because the Old Bill are bound to turn around and say, "Oh you're dealing heroin as well". So cannabis people tend to feel a lot more comfortable just dealing with cannabis people. (Male, age 45 years. Source: prison interview)

(1) Importation and wholesale

Traditionally at importation level, traffickers would have been almost wholly dealing in a single commodity – whether heroin through the Turkish route, cocaine from Colombia, or hashish from Morocco – and this underpins the importance of ethnic and kinship links already discussed. It is our impression that this remains substantially the case.

Some customs informants have stressed the increasing importance of 'cocktail' loads transported by lorry from the Continent, which will contain quantities of several commodities – ecstasy, amphetamine, heroin and cannabis. It is likely that these involve little-understood links between systems of Dutch and Belgian multi-commodity brokerage and a UK middle market broker who is thus purchasing direct rather than through UK-based upper-level importers and wholesalers.

Some of our evidence suggests that much of the 'middle market' is in fact played out in the Netherlands, Belgium and elsewhere in mainland Europe, and that this is a gap in both intelligence and enforcement operations.

Otherwise, the upper-level of importation and warehousing remains essentially a single-commodity affair. This would apply also to synthetics, whether pill factories in Holland or domestic amphetamine laboratories in the UK, which appear to be making a comeback after a period when amphetamine were predominantly imported from the Netherlands.

(2)   *Middle-level drug brokers*

A vital connection in the supply chain is the middle-level drug broker who buys in multi-kilo loads of heroin, cocaine and other substances and sells in smaller quantities – typically ounces of heroin and cocaine, part-kilos of amphetamine, kilos of cannabis and 500 to 2,000 ecstasy tablets – to customers who are either retail level dealers or the immediate suppliers to retailers.

Where these are multi-commodity drug brokers, they are highly complex and flexible business organisations – buying different substances from different suppliers who are typically mono-commodity, and selling to a wide range of customers who are also often single commodity retailers. They involve small teams, typically one man with the connections who employs maybe two or three runners. The main broker may also purchase drugs through a small network of trusted middlemen with single substance connections. They may also employ someone to warehouse drugs for them, although this might also be a trusted runner.

Detailed case studies of these kinds of drug broker network have been generated as part of this research. While they are certainly not identical, they occupy a directly similar function in the market. In some cases, more than one drug broker network of this type operated in the same vicinity, and the relationship between them was one of cooperation and not competition.

Other drug brokers occupying this position in the supply chain will deal in a more limited range of commodities. In this case, a retail dealer of heroin and cocaine will have to buy cocaine supplies from one source and heroin from another. It is not untypical for brokers with a narrower range of commodity involvement to be concerned solely with amphetamine and pills, in which case they might also be directly involved in importation from the Netherlands and elsewhere.

Drug brokers are thus positioned directly between wholesale and retail levels of drug markets. In some cases, their operations and location show how 'shallow' the chain is from importation to retail, since this can sometimes involve only four steps: importation, wholesale, broker, retailer. However, contrasting with the simplicity of this vertical supply chain, where multi-commodity drug brokers are concerned their operations involve massive horizontal complexity.

(3)   Retail-level dealers

In terms of whether they deal in one or more commodity, retailers tend to fall into three categories: (i) heavy-end single commodity heroin dealers, often supporting their own habit, and nowadays sometimes also selling crack cocaine; (ii) single commodity dealers selling mainly cannabis, also sometimes pills; (iii) multi-commodity retailers dealing largely in pills, with some amphetamine, cannabis and maybe cocaine, but rarely heroin. The third type of dealer is often closely connected to the clubbing scene.

Type (i) will tend to buy from the same supplier, as do type (ii), who operate mainly within friendship networks. Type (iii) will buy from a number of suppliers, according to price and availability. Nevertheless, customer loyalty is highly prized at all levels of the market as a form of control on supply-demand fluctuations and also on quality.

Regional variations and cross-regional networks

The existence of regional variations in the availability of some drugs, together with regional variations in retail prices, indicates that the UK does not have a national drug market. Rather, it has a series of imperfectly interlinked local and regional supply networks that also do not always resemble each other in terms of operational methods, local and historical roots, ethnic composition, etc. One question often posed is whether organised crime networks of these types are becoming less restricted in terms of geographical reach, and whether criminal networks are appearing that are truly national (and international) in character. We have a variety of information on these matters, although it is undoubtedly one of the questions that requires further in-depth research.

The parameters of drug markets do not coincide with the territories upon which British organised crime groups have traditionally been based. Traditionally, the criminal enterprise known as the 'family firm' was extremely local in its membership, composition and sphere of influence. Drug markets could never function solely on this organisational base, and it is arguably the increasing role of drugs as valued commodities within criminal enterprise that has had most influence on the changing nature of the family firm.

We have already noted some of the hybrid forms of network that have emerged within the drugs middle market, operating on a cross-regional basis while also bearing the imprint of family and kinship ties. More generally, the market has demanded that they adapt by building upon the embedded ties of family and neighbourhood to enable more businesslike, arm's length relationships in market-defined territories that were previously regarded as hostile (Hobbs 2001a). Indeed, long established family firms, some of them nationally known 'brands', were constantly referred to in law enforcement interviews, often in relation to middle market enterprises located in territories far from their home base. For instance a London family linked to dealing in Yorkshire, a Liverpool family firm linked to cocaine distribution in the North East of England, and a Yorkshire family also linked to distribution networks in the North East.

In terms of Britain's major cities, London has traditionally held a pre-eminent position in terms of the supply and distribution of drugs in the UK. There are signs that this has begun to change somewhat, although where heroin is concerned, London remains vitally important because of the networks of Turkish importers and wholesalers who predominantly live and trade in London and South East England. As a consequence, the operational effectiveness of policing directed against the heroin trade in London has implications for the whole of the UK heroin economy.

Rivalry for the status of Britain's 'second city' in drug terms probably rests between Liverpool and Manchester. It is clear from a variety of evidence that Liverpool is a city that houses a number of key drug enterprises impacting upon the rest of the country. Several of these enterprises are associated with long-standing firms that had been in existence for several generations, and that are understood by both perpetrators and law enforcement personnel as 'brand-names' to signify high levels of competence and seriousness. They have positioned themselves in the supply of ecstasy, cannabis, amphetamine, heroin and cocaine. They have links as key customers of the London-based Turkish heroin networks, and among their other business links, they purchase bulk amphetamine from a Midlands supplier to whom they also supply cannabis. However it is in the cocaine market that Liverpool criminals appear to have established a major foothold, with possibly a strategic role nationally. It is interesting that it is

Liverpool networks that have acted as brokers in the establishment of a cocaine market in the North East of England where, until very recently, cocaine was virtually unobtainable and there was little market demand. Cocaine availability has only recently become noticeable in this region, at what would appear to be a low street price of £35 per gram. Law enforcement interviews also indicated that Liverpool expertise has taken a number of forms, including the re-location of networks originating in the North West of England in areas significant to the importation of cocaine, in particular south coast ports.

While our impression of Liverpool's involvement in the middle market is one of a well established series of networked entrepreneurs operating within complex systems of brokerage, other cities assume significance due to the apparent lack of an established 'underworld'. As a result these cities are vulnerable to drug brokers who have established themselves elsewhere, and who arrive to set up new hubs and branches of their enterprise. This kind of development poses problems for law enforcement agencies that are unlikely to possess in-depth local intelligence on such transient systems.

The drugs market in other cities has been typified by multiple neighbourhood-based enterprises working in loose co-operatives, seldom involved in conflict but with good working arrangements with suppliers around the country. These, too, can find themselves vulnerable to violent predators from outside the city. In one outstanding example, these predators had been displaced from their original base by law enforcement activity, in another by violent conflict in their own city. These mobile predators either set up business on their own, or more typically they establish alliances with home-based brokers, which they can enforce because of their 'muscle power'. In a later chapter we describe how criminals with well-established violent reputations can use their potential for violence to fashion new forms of network.

A further form of variation between cities and regions is the effect of policing strategy on criminal opportunities and networks. One city was mentioned regularly as an 'open' city with no long-term family firms or 'underworld'. More recently, it had experienced considerable difficulties within the organisation of the police with the effect, some alleged, that the local drug market was largely un-policed. It was claimed that this had led to a drop in the price of heroin, not only in that city but also in the surrounding region. It had become possible for dealers and brokers around the region to collect relatively small quantities of drugs every few days and thus reduce the risks inherent in picking up large quantities every couple of weeks. It is necessary to use caution with this information, since it does not strictly accord with our more general observations on price stability, and while police in the city were sensitive to our enquiries because of their internal problems, it is also possible that other police forces in the region were seeking a scapegoat. Nevertheless, the impact on the middle market of law enforcement strategies is an important consideration. The workings of drug markets are in many ways no different from legitimate economic activities, where the lowering of trade barriers or regulatory controls would be expected to have considerable impact.

The strategic importance of geographical location in the generation of the middle market is another issue that has emerged from this initial phase of research. Indeed, some rather unusual patterns are found, which require us to understand drug markets in ways that depart from conventional, metropolitan-focused ways of thinking. For example, enforcement agencies frequently mentioned two medium-sized towns, one in the North of England and the other in the Midlands, where drug-related criminal enterprises seem to have attained a level of importance and stability that surprised us – possibly related to each town being conveniently situated close to a major port, with links by both the rail network and motorway systems to North and South, together with easy cross-country East-West motorway links. It is possible that for these kinds of reasons, seemingly unlikely locations might develop a significant role as a warehousing and distribution hub.

Ethnicity also plays its part in establishing regional variations, especially where different nationalities originate from source countries. We have already noted the controlling function of North London Turkish smugglers in the heroin trade. There are also indications of ethnic Turks located elsewhere in Britain, with links to London wholesalers and middlemen, operating as brokers in the middle market. There is also evidence that South Asians have positioned themselves in a highly profitable and strategic role in the heroin distribution system in the North of England, buying in bulk from Turks, adulterating their product four-fold and re-packaging before sale in kilo loads.

In other ways, however, the importance of ethnic links to source countries and international supply systems might be diminishing. The evidence is limited, but there are some indications that middle market drug brokers from different regions are leap-frogging the existing networks of importation and wholesale by buying direct from warehousing systems in Holland and Belgium, and importing drugs on their own behalf in smaller loads. There is some evidence that ethnic Turks are becoming reluctant to take that final step across the English Channel, preferring to sell heroin stored in mainland Europe to customers with their own transportation who are prepared to work on a 'collect' basis. These kinds of middle market 'short-cuts' are probably better established for cocaine and synthetics, and could become a growing trend. If so, then regional variations in the middle market could begin to evaporate.

5. The role of violence

Violence and a range of intimidatory devices run through the middle market like a thread. In illicit markets violence is ultimately a resource to ensure contract compliance, principally as a means of ensuring that creditors do not default on debt.

> It's part and parcel isn't it? It goes with the business. If you can't pay up for your drugs, what else can they use? (Male, age 36 years. Source: prison interview)

Many of those featuring prominently in middle market drug dealing networks bring with them prior reputations for violent action. These reputations might have been acquired through their involvement in non-drug-related activity – for instance, robbery and aggravated burglary, non-instrumental crimes such as football hooliganism, or through legitimate or semi-legitimate occupations such as bouncers or club doormen.

> I've known quite a few... the type of people you don't cross. It's a hard life, it's a dangerous business, but I've never seen people taking liberties. If you're involved in this scene you know the rules, if you break the rules you get hurt. Simple as that... it's the threat of violence that keeps people in line. (Male, age 36 years. Source: prison interview)

The potential for violence is therefore always an implied threat in such business relations, although the actual levels of violence are lower than often assumed in popular images of organised crime. Even so, there are individuals and networks within the drugs trade who will resort to extremes of physical violence, or its threat, in order to impose their will and to maintain both internal discipline and their market position.

> One established network is organised around a principle member who maintains internal discipline through both threats and actual violence. He and his group have been known at different times to use verbal threats, intimidation, assault, stabbing, kidnapping, torture and shootings in order to maintain competitiveness in the face of threats or perceived threats from rivals or associates, and in the case of jury nobbling, against members of the public. (Source: NCIS)

There were also middle market dealers, however, who made it clear that they walked away from violent conflict as a matter of business principle.

One man who worked as part of a two-man team who bought cocaine in one kilo loads and distributed this through runners in ounce and multi-ounce units said,

> It all depends how you conduct your business... I've seen people going on, "You fuckin' this, you fuckin' that, don't let me down or else bla bla bla". All we used to say was "Listen, here's what. You let me down then you don't get it again". Simple as that. Don't even come knocking on the door. But none of this I'll threaten to do this or that... That's what makes people more on edge, and if they're on edge they can do silly things... They always say don't be scared of the hard man, be scared of the frightened man... So "try to keep people sweet" I see as the best way. (Male, age 31 years. Source: prison interview)

> Yeh, you get chancers, rip-off merchants, people who fuck up with the drugs or the money... You always do in this business.... It's not worth getting involved. So a guy owes me a grand? I can turn that round in a day, no sweat, in a few hours. Why go hunting the mug down to give him a good hiding? Wasting time? Time's money, just get back to work making money. Like I say, it's not worth getting involved. (Male, age 34 years. Source: prison interview)

Overt violence within the drugs trade, as opposed to the threat of implied violence, is a category of transgression best understood as a result of *market dysfunction* and *instability*. While drug markets (i.e. supplier-purchaser relations) are functioning and drugs are being bought and sold, not only is there no need for violence because everybody involved is making money, it is to be positively avoided. Violence and killings attract police attention and leave traces, as well as attracting retaliation. Violence is therefore strictly 'bad for business'.

As one experienced middle market trader explained, who had spent 20 years in drug trafficking, purchasing as much as 100 kilos of cannabis weekly direct from importers and distributing it in smaller loads through a network of runners:

> The drugs business is a non-visible crime. As long as you're out there doing the business, nobody knows what's happening. As soon as violence or something occurs, it's brought out into the open. Big problem. That's the last thing you want.... Business has to stop. (Male, age 45 years. Source: prison interview)

This is a position quite opposed to the common reactions of politicians, the mass media and police alike who tend to regard violence as a signifier of 'gangland' organised crime, working according to principles far removed from those of orthodox economic activity

(Hobbs, 2001b). The alternative view, as advanced by Block (1983), is that an increase in violence can be an indicator that law enforcement is having a disruptive effect upon a serious network: "When networks break down through the intervention of an outside agency... information becomes a highly important and therefore dangerous commodity. In a volatile situation the key decision is whether to buy leniency or safety through informing... Increased violence is among the inevitable results." (Block, 1983: p. 235).

Illegal enterprises are unable to turn to state agencies for protection or to enforce debts (Reuter, 1983). They therefore rely on trust, albeit often reinforced by the threat of potential violence. Where trust is fragile, or where it breaks down completely, violence is then a highly valued resource that is utilised to ensure that transactions are honoured and completed. It seems more likely to be utilised in the form of intimidation, however, keeping actual levels of violence lower than often assumed in popular images of organised crime.

We find little evidence for 'turf wars' in the middle market, understood as violent conflicts over geographical territory. The notion of territory in this economic zone is largely meaningless. We have collected some testimony of localised threats and violence of this kind, but it is not conclusive and seems usually to involve relatively small-time players. Where more serious operators are concerned, their anxieties are organised around 'market territory' rather than 'geographical territory'. That is, dealers who either attempt to underprice the sale of drugs at a given level, or those who attempt to 'leap-frog' above their suppliers and to move to a higher level.

> A man who was selling several thousand ecstasy tablets per week, plus quantities of cocaine, amphetamine and cannabis, was approached by other dealers. 'They were sort of competitors, and I got warned off to be careful because I was selling the stuff so cheap... But I sold at what I thought was fair, and I was turning money round, making money. You know, if you rip people off they don't come back... But there were these other dealers, and I got warned off. The first time I didn't take no notice of it, but the second time they warned me about it... I was going to get sliced, get beaten up badly, whatever.' (Male, age 30 years. Source: prison interview)

What seems to be a recent innovation is kidnapping and hostage-taking, forms of violence that are more frequent than might be assumed, and where the victims have no interest in reporting such incidents to the authorities. Kidnapping can be seen in part as complementing the established use of violence and intimidation to counter threats to middle market competitiveness. This activity may take a number of forms. The most obvious is to enforce contractual arrangements and the payment of debts.

Examples were reported to us involving people operating at quite high levels of importation, both Colombian cocaine trafficking and Turkish control of heroin importation. Non-payment of debts had resulted either in the individual being kidnapped until family members get the money together or members of the individual's family being kidnapped until payment is made. In regard to the latter, cases have been reported of family members back in Colombia being held hostage until someone based in the UK secures the necessary funds for release. (Source: HMCE; Metropolitan Police; NCIS)

A key associate of a middle market group owed money to senior members of the group. He was met in a pub and, despite offering to pay the debt, he was taken to the countryside where he was held captive and severely beaten with both of his hands broken. He was later found, badly injured and naked, rolled up in a carpet at the back of a fish-and-chip shop. He remains part of the same middle market network. (Source: Police)

A financial dispute between an importer and a wholesaler resulted in the importer being kidnapped and held hundreds of miles from home until the debt was settled. In another case, a London-based dealer received £140,000 from a powerful family firm for a supply of heroin that was never delivered. He was kidnapped and threatened with murder if the money was not returned. The problem was eventually amicably resolved by the intervention of powerful overseas heroin suppliers. (Source: HMCE)

There are also reported cases of this kind of 'hostage taking', where motor vehicles, usually expensive four-wheel-drive models, have been captured and held until the required payment has been made.

Kidnappings can also be used as an extortion device to extract funds from rival dealers. This is not debt collection by other means, but a form of robbery against targets likely to be holding large amounts of cash and/or drugs and who are unable to turn to the police for assistance. As Jacobs (2000) has shown in his study of drug dealers as victims of robbery, dealers are highly vulnerable to this kind of attack, whether involving kidnapping or not.

A very active and successful Midlands dealer acting as a conduit for heroin importation and supplying Asian dealing networks in the North West of England was targeted by some London-based criminals. One of his houses was raided and ransacked and his partner assaulted. On this occasion hundreds of thousands of pounds were being stored in plastic bags in the attic of one of the dealer's relatives in a nearby house. (Source: NCS)

In one area of London where drugs have become a significant issue within the Bengali community, younger Bengali gangs have recognised drug dealers as lucrative targets and have become involved in arranging kidnaps. Older members of the Bengali community with established reputations are sometimes called in to resolve these conflicts. Within London's Turkish community, drug-related kidnaps are also not uncommon. In one case, two men heard on the grapevine that a known acquaintance was looking after several kilos of heroin for a third party. They visited their acquaintance, and used violence against him until he revealed where the drugs were concealed, and stole the heroin. A short time later, on learning that the third party to whom the drugs belonged was a highly respected Turkish wholesaler with a reputation for violent retribution, they returned the money that they had obtained for selling the drugs rather hurriedly. (Source: field interview; Metropolitan Police)

There are finally aspects of kidnapping and torture that, although they might target individuals who are seen to have broken 'unwritten rules', cannot be usefully understood in terms of economic rationality – either debt payment or extortion. These sometimes involve trivial sums of money, and are an intimidatory device to reinforce violent reputation.

A man who had defaulted on a drug debt was kidnapped, humiliated and tortured. The man had not owed a particularly large sum of money, and was known as something of a small-time loner who was unlikely to be able to call on 'back up' to exact retribution. He was thus a convenient target on whom to 'make an example'. He was beaten on the arms and legs with iron bars, made to dress in women's clothes and apply lipstick to himself, and various objects were inserted in his anus. Photographs were taken of his humiliating circumstances and then shown around to local people with a clear message: 'This is what happens if you mess with us'. (Source: NCS)

While this kind of theatrical violence might have an instrumental character, in reinforcing both internal and external discipline, it also has an expressive function whereby violence is celebrated as an end in itself (Katz, 1988). There is a danger in presenting violence in drug markets as purely rational, either as a means of exploiting lucrative targets for robbery or regulating an alternative economy (Furstenburg, 1969). Such a view stresses structure and hierarchy, potentially ignoring the more flexible and even chaotic nature of drug networks. When these webs of relationships are untangled, violence can often acquire personal as opposed to structural characteristics and aims. The expression of macho status within many of the environs that overlap with the drugs middle market should not be overlooked, for the middle market is a social as well as an economic system, and is based on a highly competitive mandate that pervades both the commercial and personal lives of participants.

This kind of expressive macho violence coupled with drug markets has become associated in recent years with Jamaican gangs, which are discussed below, but has a longer history in terms of white indigenous criminality (for example, the Krays). It is a point at which business principles become confused with ego. It is once again a point at which violence is a consequence not of rational attempts at the control of markets, but the breakdown of trading principles.

A note on black-on-black murders that have often been linked in public discourse with the crack cocaine market seems in order, especially in view of the high profile that these kinds of murders have assumed, chiefly in the London area. While some of these murders have involved rivals in the drug trade, the weight of evidence available to us suggests that they are more likely to be of a non-instrumental nature arising from macho cultural values and extreme sensitivities to status and 'dis-respect'. We do not wish to minimise the corrosive impact that such murders might have on the black community, or the serious impact that they have on police resources, but to define them as 'drug-related' is to misrepresent the character of drug-related violence.

It is equally important to stress that these kinds of violent machismo do not reflect any specific cultural or ethnic predisposition. Violent forms of masculinity have attracted considerable attention in recent years within criminology (Jefferson and Carlen, 1996). Values of machismo are found amongst all ethnic groups, and find expression within the drugs middle market as elsewhere, whereby perceived insults and affronts to self-esteem can lead to violence that has no economic rationality and can be entirely dysfunctional.

> Mr. G. was a middle market drug broker from a white working class background who ran a highly profitable business and had successfully circumvented law enforcement efforts in the past. For example, a couple of years ago an associate who acted as his runner had been arrested in possession of approximately £200,000 of Mr. G.'s drugs but he had bounced back. He had good working relations with dealers operating at a similar level to himself in his locality, but was involved in some kind of personal feud with a local club owner Mr. K. who had thrown Mr. G. out of one of his clubs, telling him 'You can't come here, you don't belong'. Infuriated by this insult, Mr. G. arranged for one of Mr. K.'s junior partners to be shot in the legs. In the pandemonium that ensued, several of Mr. G's associates were arrested and investigations led to the arrest of Mr. G himself, most of his other known associates and co-dealers, and the seizure of substantial quantities of drugs and cash. (Source: NCS)

In conclusion, in spite of violence being pervasive in drug markets as an implied and intimidatory force, its role should not be over-emphasised. Under normal circumstances, drug markets operate according to business principles. For example, it is frequently reported that if drugs received are not of the required standard – cannabis or ecstasy of poor quality, or amphetamine base that was too 'runny' – they will be passed back to the supplier who will rectify the situation.

There are of course 'chancers' and 'rip-off' merchants who will attempt to capitalise on the fact that drug markets are not subject to legally enforceable contracts. Examples from the field include straightforward extortion and robbery from drug dealers known to be holding large quantities of drugs or cash. Systems of 'taxing' drug dealers also exist in some localities, and this is not debt collection by other means, but an alternative to robbery. The presence of such predators lends a certain chaotic quality to drug markets that should also not be under-emphasised. Carefully organised intelligence and enforcement operations will tend to give the impression of drug market networks as tightly organised, well-run efficient organisations that are equally carefully planned. Such organisations undoubtedly exist. Interviews with imprisoned offenders, on the other hand, show how often drug networks are slipshod and also how arrests often result from carelessness, unforeseen circumstances, a departure from normal routines, and their downright bad luck.

6.   'Middlemen' and 'go-betweens': the strategic role of the middle market drug broker

We have described both the external economic environment and the broadly hierarchical structure of drug markets, and some aspects of the internal organisation of drug dealing networks. One form of network that we encountered on a number of occasions, and to which we attach special importance we will call *middle market drug brokers*. This chapter describes in more detail how this vital connecting level of the middle market operates, together with other forms of 'middlemen' and 'go-betweens'.

Middle market drug brokers

We have come across middle market drug brokers in several parts of the UK. Their operations are essentially local in scope, although their customers can sometimes make journeys of a few hours in order to purchase drugs. They supply to a regular customer base that largely involves retail dealers, or intermediaries sitting just above retail level. They purchase drugs in multi-kilo levels where heroin, cocaine, amphetamine and cannabis are concerned, and in terms of synthetics will purchase upwards of 20,000 pills on a regular basis. Some middle market brokers trade in all drug commodities, others operate within a more limited range. In more than one instance we have encountered drug brokers at this level whose main business was in cocaine, cannabis and synthetics but who were extremely reluctant, or unwilling, to deal in heroin. Others deal right across the range.

A diagrammatic representation of the strategic position of middle market drug brokers is offered in schematic form in Figure 1.

As an example of quantities and economic scale, an estimate of one middle market drug broker's shopping list every two or three weeks is as follows: two to three kilos of heroin; one to two kilos of cocaine; 30 kilos of cannabis; ten kilos of amphetamine base; 25,000 ecstasy tablets. This would entail a financial outlay over the same period in the region of £180,000 to £225,000. It is difficult to estimate the return on investment, given unknown levels of purity and adulteration, but it might amount to £300,000 to £350,000.

Middle-level drug broker networks such as this are crucial to the drug distribution enterprise. They are small in size and consist typically of a main person with the contacts to purchase

Figure 1: *Mediating role of the middle market multi-commodity drug broker*

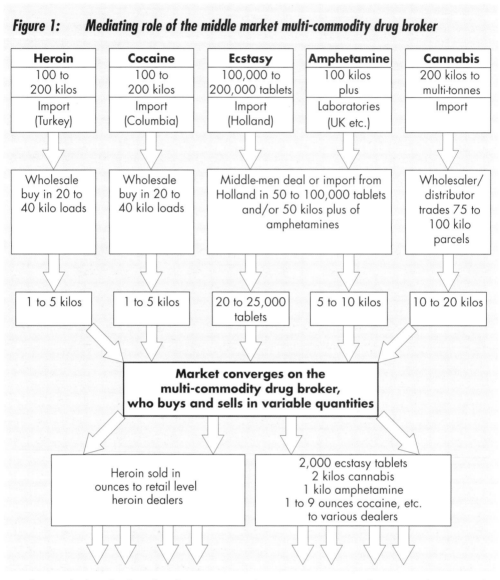

supplies and who also handles the money, and a runner or series of runners who act on his behalf – either to deliver drugs to customers, to collect drugs from suppliers and their agents, or to deliver and collect money.

In one instance two drug-brokers at more or less the same level in terms of quantities purchased were operating from the same middle-sized town, with distinct business operations, separate warehousing systems and customer relations, but often cooperating in the purchase of drugs.

Middle market drug brokers will sometimes be linked into the supply chain above them by business associates with specialised connections. For example, in the above case the two brokers collaborated in their purchases of cannabis but had to work through a third party who presumably took some form of payment for his brokerage services. Their heroin supplies appeared to be separate, although one broker bought the cutting agent (caffeine) that he used to dilute heroin from the other.

As already mentioned in an earlier chapter, where pyramid dealing hierarchies are shallow, middle market drug brokers typically sit two levels below importation and one or two above retail. We have only limited evidence of middle market drug brokers who are involved in importation, although it is clear that some teams that operate at this kind of level have direct links with intermediaries working for warehousing systems in the Netherlands, and that this might be a growing trend.

More generally, the strategic importance of their positioning is the way in which within drug markets characterised by vertical simplicity, their operations involve considerable horizontal complexity and multiple vectors linking not only different levels of the market but also different commodities from different supply sources to their varied customer bases.

Brokers and runners: partners or wage labourers?

The relations between the drug broker and his runner/s can assume a number of forms.

One variant is the form of financial arrangement between broker and runner. In one, the runner works for a consistent weekly wage, also being supplied with necessary equipment for the job, such as mobile phone and motorcar. In another he is paid per transaction, for example, £25 to deliver a kilo of base amphetamine. In a third type of relationship the runner accepts a quantity of drugs from the broker who wants a stated price back on the drugs, and the runner, in a quasi-entrepreneurial role, takes any profit that he can make over the stated price. Or, the runner might be given a small additional quantity of drugs to sell on his own behalf.

Another variant is whether or not the runner acts only on the instructions of the broker, or whether he has any independence in his actions. At one extreme, some runners are essentially entrepreneurs who generate networks of demand, first through friends and 'friends-of-friends', acting as a go-between for purchasers, taking their orders, collecting their money and obtaining quantities of drugs on their behalf from the broker. At the other extreme, the runner only supplies to customers known to him through the broker's networks, and the money will often pass by a different route. A third variation is the extent to which the runner has knowledge or sight of the extent of the broker's business.

Some brokers would have a number of people working to them, who might each occupy different roles as described above. In one case, a runner in his late teens focused solely on sales around the clubbing scene, whether direct to consumers or to lower level dealers. In the same operation, someone else dealt with heroin supplies, and the first runner had no knowledge of this side of the operation.

In a different case, a single runner handled all drug deliveries and collections for the broker on his telephoned instructions, and also stored drugs for him. This was quite an extensive business. Some of his customers were retail level heroin dealers who would purchase an ounce of heroin every day, or every two days. He would deliver kilos or half-kilos of amphetamine base to different people on a regular basis; whereas another customer would routinely purchase two to three kilos of cannabis and a couple of thousand ecstasy tablets. However, the runner had no knowledge of the financial side of the business, although he would sometimes collect and deliver cash, or hold cash on the broker's behalf. He also often knew nothing of the identities of those from whom he collected or delivered packages, other than by nicknames, by the car they would be driving, and the location at which they would meet.

In some of these cases, the relationship might look like a partnership. In one, as well as acting as runner on a payment by delivery arrangement, the runner also had his own smaller drug supply business. He was very much a minor partner, however, and there was no real sense of profit sharing. Indeed, in most if not all cases, there was little resemblance of partnership in the relations between brokers and runners. Whether it is a wage relationship or depends on the entrepreneurial flair of the runner, the affiliation is essentially exploitative.

Different types of 'middleman' linkage

It is in the very nature of drug markets, as with most other forms of commodity market, that a variety of actors find themselves in the 'middle', between an upper and a lower tier of exchange. It is only when producers sell directly to consumers (for example, small-scale market gardeners) that middlemen are not involved. Indeed, a useful way of conceptualising drug markets and the drugs business (like other kinds of business) is that they consist of a variety of levels and types of supplier/purchaser relations that are linked by different kinds of mediating agents ('middlemen' and 'go-betweens') and networks that serve different functions.

We have stressed the importance of the middle market drug broker because of the strategic position occupied between importation/wholesale and retail levels. However, it is important to stress that there are many other forms of intermediary function at all levels of the drug market, whether as a consequence of business principles or security. We can identify a number of different middleman functions. In both licit and illicit modes of business, for example, these can assume two forms.

- Middlemen who 'oil the wheels' by connecting up different links in the chain, thereby offering a service for payment. This is a classic brokerage role by which X with goods or services to supply is introduced to Y with business needs by Z who accepts a fee.

- Middlemen who position themselves strategically between a supplier and purchaser for financial gain, with the ability (and necessity) to keep these two separate. For example, Z knows X who can supply and deliver a commodity and also has connection with a potential purchaser Y. Z acts as a go-between, thus exploiting the fact that X and Y do not know each other, and his function and fee depend on this.

The second type of mediating function obviously depends on a market that is not entirely open, as with scarce commodities. In illicit markets a third kind of middleman operation occurs:

- Intermediaries are used as a means of concealment, so that the business transactions between A and B cannot be easily discovered, through the use of intermediaries C, D, E etc. This kind of compartmentalised operation is also found in licit businesses where attempts are made at various forms of tax evasion.

All three of these types and levels of mediation are found in drug markets, and are indeed essential to their operation. In some situations, however, the intermediary function serves more than one purpose. For example, a foreign European national based in Amsterdam collects on demand 30,000 to 50,000 ecstasy tablets direct from the manufacturer and sells these to a group of English drug dealers based in West Yorkshire who import these into Britain. At one level, by 'oiling the wheels' and making ecstasy available at a cheaper price than in the UK he provides a Type 1 broker service. But he also sells the tablets at twice the value that he buys them for, thus conforming to a Type 2 relationship that prevents the UK-based dealers from trading directly with the manufacturer. In all probability, however, for security reasons the manufacturer would be unprepared to deal directly with customers, so that the intermediary role also serves a Type 3 function.

This example shows one of the ways in which an individual can come to occupy a 'king-pin' mediating role between different levels of the drugs market. It also illustrates the ways in which different roles and functions interact, so that individual mediators assume multiple functions and identities, sometimes making it difficult to state with precision the position of an individual or network within a drug trafficking conspiracy. Moreover, this kind of 'off-shore' middle market operation may be increasing, thus further shortening an already-short supply chain.

7. Conclusion: a fragmented picture

The over-riding impression, both from prison interviews and interviews with enforcement personnel, is that people's perceptions of the operations of drug markets (if not drug markets themselves) are highly fragmented. No-one is able to draw the 'big picture'. This is partly a result of the actual structure of drug markets, which are constantly mutating, while also being based on different tiers of intermediaries and middlemen, and often highly compartmentalised in their organisation. It is also a consequence of some aspects of enforcement operations.

The partial and fragmented perceptions often revealed in prison interviews are hardly surprising where the 'small fry' are concerned, who are often those caught in the enforcement net. These people frequently have a very limited understanding of what they are involved in, which amounts only to their immediate environment. For example, someone might be paid a fixed amount to collect a package from X and deliver it to Y. He or she might not even be aware of the contents of the package. Someone might harbour suspicions about its contents, but is given no specific information, and does not request information since this is irrelevant to the task. Indeed, one of the unspoken rules of such relationships is that one doesn't ask too many questions.

In some cases undoubtedly, the limited accounts that offenders give of their position within a criminal network are the result of a combination of loyalty and pride ('I'm not a grass') and also fear. As discussed earlier, violence is always implicit in these relationships within illicit markets, as a means of enforcing order, financial obligations, loyalty and trust. Therefore, the inability, or unwillingness, to offer an account of other actors within a network can be a combination of actual ignorance and pretended ignorance. Even so, in analogy with conventional business, one would not expect a shop assistant serving on the counter of a branch of a national retail chain-store to understand the mechanisms of manufacture, distribution, and commodity pricing.

Quite apart from the limited knowledge of 'small-fry', at higher levels of importation and distribution, networks are often carefully compartmentalised. For example, in the case of synthetic drug production and distribution, one person is responsible for laboratory equipment, another for precursor chemicals, a third for laboratory location, a fourth for transportation, a fifth for warehousing, a sixth for arranging distribution links, and another for financial matters. In one highly organised Turkish heroin importation network described to us, different people and different premises were used to organise warehousing, financial transactions and distribution matters, as well as arrangements for collecting drug supplies from other warehousing arrangements in Continental Europe, and transporting heroin in bulk across Europe.

By means of such carefully positioned 'lieutenants', it is exceedingly difficult for enforcement agents to locate the central coordinator in such operations – if indeed there is always a centre – quite apart from how such upper tier trafficking networks inter-connect to lower tier systems of distribution and sale. Importers are careful to place 'middlemen' between themselves and lower-level purchasers, and vice versa.

The organisation of enforcement operations also contributes to this restricted vision. Enforcement operations are constrained by resources, including time and the need to get results, so that it is rarely the case that there is sufficient operational freedom to pursue links up or down the supply chain. This limited room for manoeuvre means that even the most successful operations will only provide a limited and fragmented picture of the targeted drug network, together with its supplier and customer base.

Equally, on the enforcement side the requirement not to compromise the identity of intelligence sources and informants means that only partial evidence will be sometimes presented in cases, which again produces a fragmented picture. Given that compartmentalised networks are one important aspect of drug markets, in this instance enforcement tactics and strategies 'mirror' the fragmented nature of compartmentalised drug networks.

The extent of these fragmented perceptions of drug markets and drug networks is reflected in the way in which police and customs officers engaged in intelligence work often freely admit that below a certain level they are 'un-sighted'. As often as not, limited operational resources mean that intelligence on smaller cases must be put to one side with the result that the targeted level is not far from importation, so that what happens between importation and the 'middle market' and what kinds of intermediary networks link this up to retail sale is largely an unmapped terrain. This has probably been exacerbated by the tendency for enforcement operations to move 'upstream', and on several occasions in interviews with enforcement personnel, the view was expressed that there was a growing 'void' of enforcement activity and intelligence in what might be thought of as the 'middle' of the domestic market.

Given the time constraints of our own study, it would be over-hasty to claim that the existence of this 'void' is generalised and universal. It would need a more extensive study, probably focused around force drug squads (themselves increasingly being replaced by generic serious crime units) and their activities. There may well also be regional variations in these respects. More than one source in the London region indicated that, where heroin was concerned, the intelligence available could support five times the number of operations that could be sustained by available resources. We cannot say what the picture might look like elsewhere, although given the centrality of London for the UK's systems of nationwide heroin distribution, this in itself is clearly a concern. We can only register here the anxieties expressed in interviews on many occasions, and the need for more scrutiny of this issue.

A further point has been stressed to us in numerous interviews with enforcement personnel about our fragmented understanding of the middle market. This relates to the purity of drugs at different levels of the market, and the point or points at which different drugs are bulked out with adulterants. This is highly significant for our understanding of price structures and profit margins, and there is a strong case to be made for routine and systematic purity testing of drugs seized at all levels of the market.

A related point, again stressed in interviews with enforcement and intelligence personnel, is the importance of chemical profiling or 'fingerprinting' of drugs seized. This is where the middle market offers an unrealised opportunity for intelligence gathering, which could bear significantly on our understanding of the effectiveness of high level interception efforts. Chemical profiling can identify the source country, and even the laboratory source, of heroin samples. There is a steady consensus that currently 80 to 90 per cent of heroin entering the UK is under Turkish control, and this is where intelligence efforts are targeted. It is in the nature of intelligence systems, however, that they must be highly focused, so that no-one can be entirely confident that there are not other important sources of heroin importation outside the field of vision – whether of South Asian origin, or via African, Balkan or Russian routes. Systematic chemical profiling of heroin seized at middle market levels could assist in this regard. If the source pattern of heroin seized at lower levels is the same as that seized at importation, this confirms that intelligence is broadly correct, but that part-loads are eluding enforcement efforts. However, if it should prove that samples of heroin seized (say) at ounce level do not conform to the pattern seized at importation level, this shows that there are blind-spots in the field of vision of intelligence systems focused on importation. In this way, somewhat paradoxically, the middle market can be an important source of intelligence for high-level interception efforts.

In many ways, therefore, our understanding of drug markets remains incomplete, whether in terms of intelligence and enforcement, or how a criminal network or individual is positioned within the overall market. One possible exception to these fragmented and partial viewpoints is offered by a small number of case studies gathered of single-handed operations. For example, a female heroin dealer who worked essentially to support her own drug habit, but whose business bought and sold several thousand pounds worth of heroin every week; or a fast-rising ecstasy dealer who single-handedly built up a business in a short period of time whereby he traded in several thousand tablets per week. Even so, the picture becomes blurred at the edges. The heroin dealer bought ounces from a more substantial supplier, of whose operations she had only a murky idea, while around her she had also gathered a small network of bit-part players and 'bag' sellers whose functions were not entirely clear. Whereas the ecstasy dealer generated below him a network of lower tier dealers with their own clientele unknown to him, and he was buying in bulk from intermediaries who guarded their identities, just as he never revealed his identity or his address either to them or to his customers. It comes down again to the fact that to be successful in drug dealing, an understanding of what is going on above and below you is entirely irrelevant to your commercial success.

To sum up, for a variety of reasons fragmentation appears to be a fundamental characteristic of people's perceptions of drug markets – whether these are the perceptions of participants or enforcement personnel. This was further compounded by different perceptions as to what constitutes 'the middle'. Our response in terms of methodology has been to aim for a variety of different angles and perspectives – those of people above (whether offenders or enforcement officers) looking down; people below looking up; people looking from the periphery of a network inwards; people at the centre of a network looking outwards, etc. This means that the picture is rather like a large jigsaw – but a jigsaw in which each particular piece comes from a different set.

Appendix

Case studies and vignettes

Case study 1: Turkish heroin importation and wholesale networks

It is generally agreed from intelligence sources, that Turkish networks dominate the transportation and importation of bulk loads of heroin of 100 kilos or more. These networks vary in terms of sophistication and organisation, but are generally quite small and tightly organised around kinship. Some have been identified as having a strict division of labour among the major players in terms of finance, transport, warehousing and customer relations, using different premises for different aspects of the business. Others seem less well-organised.

London is the centre of these Turkish networks, although bulk loads of heroin are often warehoused in Continental Europe, and part loads can be purchased on a 'collect' basis. Smaller quantities of 20 to 30 kilos will be stored in the London region, with a variety of different distribution systems to other parts of the UK. Below this level are a variety of bit-part players within the Turkish community, who work on a casual basis for different wholesalers at different times, depending on who is holding drugs and needs their services.

- Mr. A has purchased a 20 kilo load of heroin which is stored in a flat where it is guarded by his cousin, Mr. B. On Mr. A's instructions, Mr. B will deliver loads of one or two kilos to customers. This 'baby-sitting' arrangement might take a week or two to complete. At other times, Mr. B has worked on a similar basis for Mr. C, to whom he is not related.

- Mr. D and his junior partner/driver, Mr. E, regularly purchased heroin from a London-based Turkish dealer. They received instructions to drive a van to a location where they were met by a go-between, Mr. F. F then took the van and drove it to a warehouse and loaded several kilos of heroin, while D and E awaited his return. The money was paid to another go-between, Mr. G. F and G worked for Mr. H, who was the importer, and who employed I and J as drivers to collect from Europe. The warehouse was guarded by K who was Mr. H's nephew. On each occasion, D and E were instructed to meet F at different locations.

- Three white males from the Merseyside region travelled to London by train and were met at the railway station by three Turkish males. A sports bag containing £80,000 was handed over to the Turks, in exchange for a bag containing four kilos of heroin. The men then took the train home.

- Steve, in his mid-40s, was a career criminal who had spent a lifetime in drugs and crime. Throughout the 1990s he was involved in heroin, and for some years he bought from a Turkish connection in north London. He was trading one to two kilos per week at £21,000 per kilo, and selling in ounces, multi-ounces and part-ounces at £800 to £1,000 per ounce. He always bought from the same source. Heroin was being imported in 20 to 30 kilo loads, and he might be allowed to buy a part-load of five kilos. 'Obviously, I say the same source, I never met the man. My person was the person who just sat in-between, contacted the Turk... it was mostly Turkish.'

- A small group of Pakistani males in the north of England regularly bought three to four kilos of good quality heroin from a Turkish connection in London. They adulterated this three- or four-fold, then re-packaged the heroin in one kilo parcels using a press, and sold to customers 'as new'. The group had previously been involved in importation from Pakistan, but found the new arrangement both less risky and more profitable.

(Source: HMCE; Metropolitan Police; NCS; NCIS; prison interviews)

Case study 2: Asian heroin importation and national distribution networks

Although a very large proportion of heroin imported into Britain is nowadays under Turkish control, there is also a continuing involvement of South Asian networks from the Indian subcontinent.

One such network was compact and family-based and consisted of second-generation Pakistani UK residents, working to an uncle who was first generation, and other elder members of the kinship group resident in both Pakistan and the UK. In all there were five or six people involved.

They imported heroin in ten to 15 kilo loads by air through couriers recruited in Pakistan. After one courier panicked and left the baggage at the airport, transport systems were changed. Baggage handlers at a UK airport were recruited to intercept the suitcase at arrival and to arrange for it to be removed from the aeroplane and to circumvent customs. For this service, the corrupt baggage handling team, who were white, would be paid £5,000 per kilo, and they generally held back half of the load until they were paid. Couriers were still recruited in Pakistan, although this new arrangement meant that the courier took very little risk, because his/her job was simply to get the suitcase onto the plane. The new transport system was very difficult to coordinate, however, because the suitcase had to get onto a plane in Pakistan, which would arrive to coincide with the shift-working system of the baggage team.

In terms of prices, they were buying heroin in Pakistan at £2,000 per kilo and selling in the UK for £14,000 to £16,000 per kilo. The heroin was poor quality. A load therefore might cost anything between £30,000 to £40,000 and would be sold for £220,000 to £280,000. Even after paying the baggage handlers, profits would be in the region of £120,000 to £150,000 per load. Their distribution system was to Pakistani dealers and low-level distributors in a number of towns and cities scattered across the UK who would typically buy one to two kilos.

(Source: HMCE)

Case study 3: heroin cross-regional distribution network

Mr. W was a man of African-Caribbean descent who established a heroin-dealing network with contacts in different parts of England. He had discovered the profitability of heroin while serving a prison sentence for living on immoral earnings. 'They were turning £700, £800 out of an eighth of heroin [3.5 gms.] and to me that was big money... All I could see was £ signs, it was just too much money to let it go. So I started when I came out.' People were prepared to pay as much as £1000 for an ounce of heroin, and Mr. W found that he could buy for £700 or less. At first he was turning over an ounce a day, but he was soon buying kilo loads and selling half of a 'nine-bar' per day. He paid approximately £17,500 per kilo and at his peak he was selling five kilos per week. He had four women working for him who were each paid £1,500 per week for collecting and delivering parcels of heroin to his five main customers who were based in Manchester, Southampton, Bristol and London. This network was based on old friends and family members who happened to live in these different cities. The financial arrangements were that if he bought one kilo from his supplier, then he would receive another kilo on a credit basis, and he would do the same to his customers who were taking nine-bar and half-kilo loads on a regular basis. Mr. W also bought and sold smaller amounts of cocaine, although this was mainly because he liked to smoke crack 'as a treat'. He reckoned that an ounce of crack cocaine costing £1,000 would sell for £3,500 on the basis of six or seven £20 'stones' per gram. He was not particularly interested in this retail trade, however, and his main business remained heroin, which funded a lavish lifestyle for himself and his extended family. Mr. W knew other small networks that were buying heroin in Amsterdam for £8,000 per kilo and importing it through body-packing. As for his own position in the market, Mr. W said 'I never liked to think of myself as the boss... People used to think I'm the boss, and OK I'm that, but I said to myself they should see some of the blokes who I'm dealing with, blokes who I'm giving seventy grand to twice a week, and I'm not his best customer.'

(Source: prison interview)

Case study 4: ecstasy importation and regional distribution network

Mr. A was based in a Yorkshire city where he owned a couple of clubs and other property. He also had a drugs business that involved receiving imported loads from Holland and distributing them both within the city, and also to other cities such as Liverpool and Glasgow. The main business was ecstasy, and he distributed approximately 20,000 to 30,000 tablets per week. He also had a more limited business in cannabis and cocaine, but never traded in heroin. He had two people working for him, B and C, distributing drugs to smaller dealers in the city, one of whom was black and who had been recruited specifically to liaise with African-Caribbean dealers who had previously threatened violence and attempted to 'tax' A's other runner. Known customers would also travel from Glasgow, Liverpool and elsewhere to collect drugs from A, which they received on a credit basis. The financial side of these transactions was always handled by A, but after he lost his driving licence, an old school friend (D) started working for the firm, driving to Glasgow and Liverpool to collect money which was due one week after the drugs had been received. D sometimes travelled with Mr. A, sometimes alone, but he never touched drugs and handled only money. The transport arrangements from Holland were handled for Mr. A by someone else who was unknown to B and C. In all, Mr. A's firm traded with about a dozen lower level dealers, who would buy two to three thousand ecstasy tablets and a few ounces of cocaine when this was available. Buying at £1 per tablet and selling at £2.50 to £3, this side of Mr. A's business made £50,000 per week, although his overheads were considerable. If he could obtain one kilo of cocaine per week at the right price and quality, he could make a further £20,000 profit with minimal additional overheads, but this was not always possible through his Dutch connections.

(Source: prison interview)

Case study 5: Jamaican cocaine smuggling and crack distribution

One form of cocaine smuggling, typically using couriers from the Caribbean, involves gangs of Jamaican origin. These are also implicated in the production and distribution of cocaine in its 'crack' or 'rock' form. Some examples can describe their mode of operation.

- One London operation involved two black British men with links to Jamaica. They employed a number of couriers, recruited among people known to them through the club scene, and cocaine was imported in 15 kilo loads. Their Jamaican contacts were high level, and they received the cocaine on credit, the cash being returned within one week. On arrival in London, the cocaine was immediately 'washed up' and then delivered in two seven kilo parcels to a middleman in Bristol who himself had three or four people working under him. The men paid about £12,000 per kilo for the cocaine, and were selling at £18,000 to £20,000, a profit of approximately £100,000 per load.

- Kevin had worked for some time as the 'runner' for a middle market drug broker, Mr. T, in a southern provincial town. One of Mr. T's suppliers was a London-based Jamaican network. Mr. T suggested to Kevin that they should take up the offer of a holiday in the Caribbean and 'bring something over' for which he was told they would be paid £5,000 each (which sounds excessive). They spent two weeks in Jamaica, met various people, and were given a suitcase that Kevin would carry back. He did not know how the drugs had been packed into the suitcase, but a search by Customs officers in the UK revealed half-a-dozen bottles of Red Stripe beer containing cocaine in liquid form and some tourist souvenir vases with false bottoms also containing cocaine, together valued at £120,000.

- Sally and Lucy had been approached with the promise of a free Caribbean holiday, although they had no previous experience of drug dealing. They were required to bring back a suitcase each, did not know what these contained but believed it might be gold. They were instructed not to open the suitcases, but Sally opened hers while still at the hotel, found packages of white powder and abandoned it. Lucy carried hers onto the aeroplane, but panicked on arrival at London airport and left it on a baggage carousel. They went to the police and told their story. A week later there was an arson attack at Sally's flat.

- Pete was offered a free Caribbean holiday and a cash payment at a time, as he put it, when 'I was down on my luck'. It was his first and only involvement in drug dealing. Both he and his travelling companion were searched on their return by Customs, and were found to have six kilos of cocaine carefully concealed inside their suitcases. 'I was just the puppet', said Pete, 'It was tempting, but I didn't think, I was really stupid.'

(Source: HMCE; Metropolitan Police; prison interviews)

Case study 6: cannabis regional distribution network and wholesaler

Mr. M was in his mid-40s and had been in the cannabis trade for 20 years and ran a regional distribution network in south west England and Wales. He bought direct from importers, and typically bought and sold 70 to 100 kilos of cannabis per week. The price varied according to whether or not he received the drugs on a three-week credit basis when he might pay £1,500 per kilo. (The price of cannabis at this level of the market has recently fallen below this.) Working on a high turnover, small profit basis he would expect to add £25 to £50 per kilo, depending on quality. This could yield £3,000 to £4,000 profit per week, minus overheads. He operated a builder's yard as a front for the business, which he said he ran at a loss. There were half-a-dozen men working directly below him, comprising his distribution network, to whom he would lay on five to ten kilo parcels. Mr. M bought from three of four different importers, according to availability, price and quality. 'A typical load for them', he said, 'would be three to four tons. Three tons sounds like a lot of hash, but it'll disappear, thin air, gone. Three or four busy guys like me working off a three–ton parcel, you'd make that disappear within six weeks, two months.' If two importers had cannabis available at the same time, Mr. M might get a load on credit from one supplier that he would sell immediately intact at a minimal profit of £10 per kilo, and then use the money from that deal to buy from the second supplier at a cheaper price in a cash transaction. 'You've got to be sharp', he said 'It's a business like any other. But if you're turning money over, and to importers that's the number one priority, then you can get a keen price... You're giving him £600,000, £700,000 a month, that guy wants you, he's looking for you in the firm, 'cos you're turning money over fast.'

Mr. M traded only in cannabis, although he recognised the profits were higher in class A drugs. 'You could buy a kilo of coke, a pack not powder, solid, for £25 to £27,000, which is a realistic price. Split that into ounces, sell it at £1,000 an ounce. Don't play with it, don't do nothing with it, don't cut it... percentage is everything in the coke business, if it's been messed about with then it's crap... You would turn that out in a week. £35,000 on a kilo of charley, how much dope would you have to sell, how many units would you have to shift to make the same money?'

'Even the fellers bringing it in, they're not gonna be doubling their money any more... I said to a guy this morning, who knows the game, and I said to him, "Hash is finished, the game's done in". It's all down to skunk now of course.'

(Source: prison interview)

Case study 7: high-flying ecstasy dealer

Paul was a young man in his mid-20s who liked to go clubbing at the weekend with friends. On one occasion they bought some ecstasy tablets in a club that proved to be duds. Paul wondered whether he could buy some of better quality outside the club scene, found that he could and bought a few for his friends. In following weeks, his friends asked him to repeat this, and subsequently, as Paul described it, 'It just went on from there. You know, then their friends want, and their friends want and then it's just escalated... and eventually you've got other people who want to start dealing and then dealers buy from you, and it's a sky rocket before you even know it.' Within a matter of months, from a standing start, Paul was a substantial middleman dealer, selling two to three thousand ecstasy tablets per week, plus a few ounces of cocaine and amphetamine, and a couple of kilos of cannabis. Initially, when he was just buying for a circle of maybe 30 friends, he could buy tablets in multiples of 100 for £5 each and sell them for £7.50, at a time when the club retail price was £12. Later, when he was buy thousands he could obtain these for £2.50 to £3 each, and sold to second-tier dealers below him for £5 each per 100 tablets. He worked single-handed and was very well organised. He 'went shopping' for his drugs at the start of each week, took orders in mid-week, and delivered before the weekend. He was arrested quite accidentally following a routine road traffic check.

(Source: prison interview)

Case study 8: cocaine and crack ounce dealers

Kenny and Keith were in their mid-20s when they came to London from the Liverpool area, looking for work. They had dabbled in drugs before, 'bibs and bobs of cannabis mainly', said Kenny. Living just outside London, they started to mix with a group of friends who snorted cocaine at the weekends, each putting a quantity of money into a pot and buying cocaine to share. Kenny remembers that as the circle of friends grew – 'friends of friends, and that kind of thing' – the arrangement became more formal and businesslike.

At first Kenny and Keith were buying an ounce and cutting and weighing that into grams. Then they began buying quarter-kilo 'nine-bars' of cocaine, and later they were buying kilos and selling in ounce and multi-ounce deals. They found both that there was a growing demand for 'rocks', and that the business was much more profitable if they 'washed' the powder cocaine and sold as rocks. They also started smoking rocks themselves, which cut into their profit margins, although Kenny said 'We always stayed on top, we were making loads of money'. Eventually they had a network of runners working for them.

Kenny said it took about six months to the stage where they were buying cocaine by the kilo. They had two suppliers, the most consistent of whom was a club owner who charged £25,000 for a kilo and £7,500 for a nine-bar. It was always good quality, which the club owner referred to as 'Columbia flake', and Kenny and Keith sold it without cutting agents and never had any complaints from customers. Kenny reckoned that if half a kilo was washed up, the profit from that would pay for the whole kilo: 'The rest was profit, or "our smoke", as we used to say.'

Kenny and Keith never had customers calling at their home, and moved their location frequently. 'If someone wanted an ounce, two ounces of charley or rock, we'd deliver in person... But we had to know them well. The lads we used as runners, we'd give them ten £20 rocks, £50 rocks, and say, "Sell that, keep two for yourself." We never had direct dealings with crack heads, they're a liability.'

Prices sometimes varied, but Kenny and Keith always sold at the same price. Their supplier would sometimes take as little as £20,000 for a kilo if he wanted to turn it over quickly. At other times the price would be higher, but these higher costs were not passed on to the customer. 'Like, you take an ounce of charley, might cost you £800, wash it up you'll get back £4,000 to £5,000... With money like that you don't need to be fussy, you're always gonna be on top.'

(Source: prison interview)

Case study 9: Dutch-based foreign national broker

Alfonso was a Dutch-based drug broker in his late-30s, who had served a prison sentence in Germany in the past for his role in drug trafficking. He traded mainly in ecstasy, where he was well connected, and also in cocaine, although he viewed this as less profitable. He purchased drugs for his customers on demand and usually had half-a-dozen that he traded with at any one time. One of his customers was a British-based gang working in the Yorkshire area who requested 30,000 ecstasy tablets and one kilo of cocaine on a regular basis. He bought the tablets from a man who himself purchased direct from the manufacturer, and who Alfonso reckoned bought 600,000 tablets every three or four days. Alfonso bought at approximately 0.50p per tablet and sold them to the British people for £1 each. They also wanted to buy more cocaine from him, but he found this less profitable since he could buy one kilo of cocaine at £13,000 to £14,000 but could only expect to sell it for £16,000 to £17,000. He also found that the price for cocaine was unstable. Alfonso always worked alone. 'There was so much involved', he said, 'I used to spend everything... a nice lifestyle, holidays... and then do it again... There's lots of people want drugs. You want it, I can get it. I was more or less a middle man.'

(Source: prison interview)

Case study 10: provincial town, multi-commodity drug broker's runner

Alf worked for a man named Mr. R who was one of a small number of multi-commodity drug brokers in an area of the North West of England, supplying drugs to people in nearby towns and sometimes as far away as Birmingham or Wales. Alf and R were the same age and had known each other since childhood. Alf, who worked in the building trade, started working for R when his previous 'dealer' had been arrested while in possession of £100,000 of R's drugs. He had never been involved in drug dealing before, and R explained to him that his job would involve collecting and delivering drugs of different types – cocaine, heroin, ecstasy, cannabis, amphetamine. Alf was paid £300 per week. Mr. R also supplied a car and a mobile phone.

Alf collected and delivered drugs to different people at different times, often to regular customers. For example, he delivered to a female heroin dealer who took one ounce of heroin every two days; this woman also sometimes tested the quality of heroin for Mr. R. Another regular customer was a man from near Liverpool who took four to five kilos of cannabis every two to three weeks plus 1,000 ecstasy tablets. He usually met customers such as these in pub car parks, or in the car parks of supermarkets or roadside restaurants such as the Little Chef or Pizza Hut. A man called B who was the uncle of one of R's associates took one kilo of amphetamine base every two weeks; and also he delivered to C, who was R's cousin, who had ounces of heroin on a regular basis. Another man called D received a dozen nine-bars of cannabis every two weeks, and Alf used to meet F from Birmingham in a pub car park every couple of weeks and supply him with three kilos of cannabis bush [grass] and 1000 ecstasy tablets. In addition to these regular customers, there were times when Alf dealt with people who were unknown to him on the instructions of R. For example, on one occasion he met two men in a red car at a designated lay-by and handed over one kilo of amphetamine base, and a few days later he met another man in a white estate car to whom he delivered four nine-bars of cannabis.

Although Alf also sometimes collected and delivered money on R's behalf, he knew little about the financial side of the business – this was handled by R. Alf stored drugs for R at his own house, and in a garage lock-up. Mr. R also stored drugs at the house of a close family member where he would mix heroin that he had bought with 'bash' in the form of paracetamol, using kitchen equipment. In quantity terms Alf reckoned that each month R handled ten kilos of amphetamine, 15 kilos of cannabis, 25,000 ecstasy tablets, two kilos of heroin and a kilo of cocaine on a less regular basis. Another man in the same town, with whom R sometimes cooperated, was trading in similar amounts, although much larger quantities of cannabis. Alf reckoned that he collected or delivered from 30 people or more, and on occasions he also collected and delivered guns from one or another of R's associates.

(Source: prison interview; NCS)

Case study 11: middle market 'runners' and 'gofers'

We have identified middle market drug brokers as occupying a key role in the distribution chain. These were essentially small networks, and the core member would have one or more 'runners' working to him. One such arrangement is described in detail in case study 10, and case study 13 also describes a retail heroin dealer's relationship with her supplier, who used a team of runners. These relationships can take different forms.

Mr. P operated from one of the orbital towns around London, and traded in all of the most common illicit drugs – cocaine, cannabis, amphetamine, ecstasy, and occasionally heroin – although he was sometimes reluctant to get involved in heroin. Mr. P worked with two trusted colleagues, of whom Mr. Q was the most active. As Mr. P's agent, Q would collect and deliver quantities of different drugs, and he was paid for each delivery or transaction. On this basis, P supplied to six or seven dealers in two nearby towns who themselves supplied a network of pubs, clubs and other locations. Mr. Q also had his own sideline business, which was known to Mr. P, with his own network of runners and dealers. The relations between P and Q were therefore fluid, but not equal. For example, on one occasion Q purchased some 'fake' ecstasy tablets – possibly amphetamine plus ketamine – and supplied these to customers of P, who complained. P told Q to sort out his suppliers, and 'Don't do it again'.

In terms of quantities, P would typically and routinely sell ten kilo loads of cannabis, ounces of cocaine and several thousand ecstasy tablets per transaction. He did not particularly like dealing in heroin, although he could be persuaded to supply half to one kilo on demand to relatively new customers, and up to five kilos if someone were known to him. He was busier with cocaine. Although Mr. P and Q were regular associates, P did not particularly trust Q. Although Q would routinely handle cash for P, in a larger deal involving maybe £20,000 to £40,000, P would want to be 'hands on'.

By contrast, Micky was very much a junior partner in his relations with the man whom he called the 'Guv'. Nineteen years of age and living in a southern coastal town, Micky said that he liked being involved in drugs because 'It gave me a buzz, I was someone to look up to... I could always get hold of whatever people wanted... people would say, "Oh, look at him". I was happy about that... I suppose I just wanted to get a name for myself.' Micky also had a job doing bar work, which meant that he met a lot of people. Effectively, he recruited customers on behalf of the 'Guv', and found that it was easiest to sell ecstasy. He reckoned that he had sold as many as 10,000 pills in a week. His payment came in the form of drugs, in that he could always 'skim' a few from any deal that he was involved in.

The 'Guv' never gave him drugs on credit. Micky always had to have cash in hand from his customers. Micky knew nothing about the financial side of the business, although he knew that the 'Guv' had a number of other gofers, dealing in heroin and crack cocaine among other things.

The nature of these relationships is often, perhaps invariably, exploitative. Joey was someone who was 'streetwise', and a regular user of cannabis, powder cocaine and amphetamine. But he had a sober view of the casual labour market in the middle market drugs trade. 'The risks are too big', he said, 'and the money's not that brilliant. One geezer I knew was dropping off 'ozzies' [ounces of cocaine] for this other feller, and he was getting paid £25 for each package... 25 quid, that's fuck all. Alright, he's maybe doing, 10, 20, 25 a week... that's maybe three hundred, a monkey [£500] in his hand.... But he's not doing them one by one, you know what I mean, he's always carrying, I don't know, five or seven ounces at any one time... And if it all comes on top, he's the one in the firing line, no-one else.... and seven ounces of cocaine, you're looking at fucking serious bird.... It's not for me.'

(Source: prison interview; NCS; field interview)

Case study 12: importation and regional distribution of ecstasy and amphetamine

Ronnie and Terry had been good friends since their schooldays in a middle-sized town in the East Midlands, where they lived on a run-down council estate. In the past, as ardent supporters of their local football team, they had been heavily involved in football hooliganism and enjoyed a fearsome local reputation.

Ronnie and Terry formed the hub of a small crime network, importing ecstasy, amphetamine and occasionally cannabis from Holland and supplying a network of dealers in two nearby cities. Ronnie took responsibility for storing the drugs, financial matters, and was sometimes involved in distribution. Terry took responsibility for collecting drug loads in the UK. There were a couple of other associates who would deliver drugs to their customers.

The gang had two regular suppliers, both in Holland, but with different transport systems. One would deliver to an agreed location in England; the other required someone to collect from Holland. In the first case, a lorry would be driven to a nominated town from where the drugs were collected and taken to their base. In the second case, couriers would be sent to collect the drugs from Holland and bring these back to England, where they would be met at a railway station to hand over their bags.

In terms of quantities, they worked in loads of 10 to 15 kilos and sometimes as much as 40 kilos, every two to three weeks. If he found himself short of drugs, Ronnie would buy from competitors in the two nearby cities in order to supply his customers in those places. They had approximately six regular customers. Prices could vary. For example, they increased sharply for a period after a Dutch-based lab had been put out of action by enforcement efforts. However, these extra costs were absorbed by the network and not passed on to customers. The gang are very conscious of law enforcement efforts, and following the arrest of one of the junior partners they were momentarily thrown into disarray while they changed their transport systems, routes and routines, and lorry drivers.

Violence was rare, although always implied if someone stepped out of line or failed to deliver on debts. The network members were regularly involved in punch-ups in pubs. These were not drug-related, although they helped to maintain the gang's local reputation.

(Source: HMCE)

Case study 13: busy retail-level heroin user-dealer

User-dealers are often depicted as the bottom rung of the ladder. However, they are sometimes well organised and occupy an important and profitable position in the heroin trade.

Helen was a woman in her twenties who found that dealing in the drug was the easiest way to manage her prodigious heroin habit. She bought, on average, one ounce of heroin each day for £850 (equivalent to £30 per gram) from a multi-commodity broker in a nearby town, and this was sold in £20 bags. He also asked her whether she would like to deal in cocaine, but she was not interested: 'I only done what I done with heroin because I needed it... I didn't have a cocaine habit, so what was the point? I only probably would have ended up with one if I'd agreed to it.' Helen had two people who sold the bags on her behalf on the street, and she was happy if she got £1,150 back from the ounce, which gave her £300 profit. She did not bother adding any cutting agent to it, which was more trouble than it was worth, and, if she was busy, there were a couple of people whom she trusted who would do the bagging up for her. They would be paid for their work either in cash or in heroin. 'Whatever they wanted... at least two grams. I would supply it and they would use it. It was there basically.' The fundamental business principle of this operation was Helen's heroin habit, but she could not estimate how much she used: 'I was smoking quite large quantities. I couldn't actually put an amount on it because I was getting it in any amount. I was just, I was just greedy basically with my habit.'

In addition to Helen's personal consumption, and that of the friends who bagged up for her, there were probably other friends and hangers-on. Depending on the quantity of heroin in the £20 bags (and it can vary regionally from 0.2 grams to almost half a gram), Helen and her friends must have been smoking at least 20 per cent of the heroin that she purchased and possibly more, in addition to the £300 per day cash profit that she made.

(Source: prison interview)

Case study 14: middle market ounce-broker in heroin and cocaine

Mr. H was another heroin user who ran a profitable drugs business, even though he estimated that he consumed £2,000 worth of heroin and £1,000 of cocaine each week, while remaining in full-time employment as a media consultant. Now aged 30, he had started off just selling to friends, but he said 'It kind of escalates quite easily... especially on the clubbing scene... it gets around that you can sort people out for drugs, and friends of friends... that sort of thing.' He had first used heroin to relax and 'come down' after a weekend clubbing, but found that he started smoking more and more. His drug dealing grew proportionately.

Mr. H would buy drugs from two regular suppliers on a weekly basis. Living in an East Midlands town, he travelled to London to buy cocaine from people whom he knew well, and he purchased heroin from suppliers in Merseyside, whom he described as 'very wealthy drug dealers' who were 'one step, maybe two down from the people who were bringing it into the country'. For his Merseyside connection, he would either meet a courier half-way or arrange for it to be delivered to him. Mr. H estimated that the people in London were doing between six to ten deals of the same sort of size as his own each week, or roughly three kilos of cocaine per week, although occasionally they would supply a load as big as ten kilos. His Liverpool suppliers were strictly 'hands off' and did not use drugs, but he thought they were selling at least ten kilos of heroin a week. He had made contact with the Liverpool connection through a friend who had gone to prison, and who gave him an introduction with a 'reference' as a reliable man who could handle the amounts that his friend had been dealing.

Mr. H bought roughly a quarter of a kilo of cocaine per week, and a quarter to a half kilo of heroin, plus a sideline of 500 to 1,000 ecstasy tablets each week from a friend in his home town. He paid £8,000 for nine ounces of cocaine, which he sold for £1,200 per ounce – an overall profit of approximately £2,000 per week. He bought heroin at £5,500 for a quarter-kilo 'nine-bar', that is £600 per ounce, which he said was 'a good price', and he was selling heroin for anywhere between £900 and £1,000 per ounce. Cocaine could be obtained more cheaply, but not at the purity that he was buying. He never tampered with the drugs, since he was dealing to friends. Mr. H sold heroin mainly to a network of five or six people, and cocaine to four or five people, although there were a couple of dozen friends that he would 'sort out' if they wanted small amounts at any time. His typical heroin customers bought half ounce and ounce amounts upwards; his cocaine customers bought quarter-ounces upwards. The people to whom he was selling did not in any sense work for him, 'Towards the end it mostly went in big-ish amounts to a few friends and who they sold to it was, you know, their business.... I suppose it was sort of people-who-knew-people.' He contrasted this with dealers who operate a network: 'I didn't so much have people distributing for me... like some people have you know a little network, they have people who do jobs for them.... But I was pretty much my own person.'

(Source: prison interview)

Case study 15: amphetamine dealing: different markets; different levels

Luke was in his early-30s and had a lucrative business in amphetamine, ecstasy and cocaine. Where amphetamine was concerned, a young woman worked to him who could distribute a kilo per month. Luke bought at £3,000 per kilo and the selling price was £220 per ounce (equivalent to £7,800 per kilo) – a profit of almost £5,000. This was 'base' amphetamine of high purity that, sold uncut, would cost £20 per gram, which involves a further doubling up of money for those people buying ounces and selling grams. Luke also had three customers who required 1,000 ecstasy tablets per month. He could buy these at £2.25 to £3.00 each and added 0.75p to the price, which yielded a further £2,250 profit per month. In addition, Luke bought one ounce of cocaine per week for £950 that he sold for £65 to £70 per gram, adding roughly £1,000 profit. He sometimes sold at £200 for an eighth of an ounce (equivalent to £56 per gram), and had customers who asked if he could get them ounces, but he refused to become further involved in the cocaine trade because of the penalties that might be incurred if he were arrested.

Luke reckoned that he had no more than ten direct customers at any one time. He made it clear that the market for base amphetamine was quite distinct from that for 'speed' or 'whizz', typically sold in gram units as one of the recreational 'dance drugs' around the club scene. 'By the time it gets to your £8 wrap', he said, 'it's been cut and cut and cut – half is glucose, and what the other half is, that's debatable.'

This was also Dave's view, who operated at a lower level of the base amphetamine market. Dave bought at £200 an ounce (equivalent to £7 a gram), sometimes less, and sold for £15 a gram although he knew people who charged £20. He refused to buy amphetamine unless it was 'untouched' in a sticky form, which he likened to 'a block of icing sugar', a texture that Luke described as 'waxy chalk'. Dave would sometimes add ten per cent glucose before selling, but this was simply to make the product into a snortable powder, rather than to add to his profits.

A further example indicating variations in price and purity within this market is Polly, who started dealing amphetamine in her late teens around the club scene in a southern coastal town. She began in a small way but in what seems like quite a typical pattern around the club drug scene, once involved in drug dealing, her scale of operations expanded rapidly. 'Once I started, other people got to hear and that type of thing, and it escalates very quickly. I mean in the end, we're talking about like 1,000 tablets a week and like nine ounces of amphetamine... As soon as it started, phew, it got out of control really.' Polly paid £450 for nine ounces 'pretty pure', which she sold for £250 per ounce having used mixing agents to bulk out the product by a factor of two. She was selling to people who would themselves add further mixing agents to the product, which is why she did not dilute it further. Even so, on this basis her outlay of £450 yielded a profit of approximately £4,000. In addition, she was also buying 1,000 ecstasy pills at 0.75p to £1 per tablet, maybe £1.50 if they were good quality. These she sold in batches of 100 for £3 to £5 per tablet depending on how well she knew the purchaser, so that for each load she was making between £3,000 to £4,000 profit.

In one further twist, Polly reached agreement with a club owner for 'exclusive rights' in his establishment. She already knew the door staff and bar staff, paying them off in drinks and drugs, so that it was a natural progression to formalise the arrangement. The club owner accepted £500 per week for his compliance. Polly was now a well-established, middle-level dealer, but even so admitted that it was both greedy and risky when she decided to continue selling direct to punters in clubs. She would regularly carry 200 tablets per night into clubs, selling at £10 each, and making almost £2,000 clear profit on top of her already lucrative business. 'I was greedy', Polly said, 'out of my depth.'

(Source: prison interview; field interview)

Adler, P.A. (1985) *Wheeling and Dealing: An Ethnography of an Upper-Level Drug Dealing and Smuggling Community.* New York: Columbia University Press.

Adler, P.A. (1992) 'The "Post" Phase of Deviant Careers: Reintegrating Drug Traffickers', *Deviant Behavior*, vol. 13, pp. 103-126.

Albanese, J. (1996) *Organised Crime in America (3rd edition).* Cincinnati: Anderson.

Arlacchi, P. (1986) *Mafia Business: the Mafia Ethic and the Spirit of Capitalism.* Oxford: Oxford University Press.

Barnes, T., Elias, R. and Walsh, P. (2000) *Cocky: The Rise and Fall of Curtis Warren.* Bury, Lancashire: Milo.

Baron, S. and Tindall, D.B. (1993) 'Network Structure and Delinquent Attitudes within a Juvenile Gang', *Social Networks*, vol. 15, no. 3, pp. 255-273.

Bean, J.P. (1981) *The Sheffield Gang Wars.* Sheffield: D & D Publications.

Berkowitz, S.D. (1982) *An Introduction to Structural Analysis: The Network Approach to Social Research.* Toronto: Butterworth.

Block, A. (1983) *East Side-West Side: Organising Crime in New York, 1930-1950.* Newark, NJ: Transaction.

Bourgois, P. (1995) *In Search of Respect: Selling Crack in El Barrio.* Cambridge: Cambridge University Press.

Caulkins, J.P. (1994) *Developing Price Series for Cocaine.* Santa Monica: RAND.

Chin, K.L. (1990) *Chinese Subculture and Criminality: Non-traditional Crime Groups in America.* New York: Greenwood Press.

Coles, N. (2001) 'It's Not What You Know, It's Who You Know: Analysing Serious Crime Groups as Social Networks', *British Journal of Criminology*, vol. 4, no. 41, pp. 580-594.

Crane, B.D., Rivolo, A.R. and Comfort, G.C. (1997) *An Empirical Examination of Counterdrug Interdiction Programme Effectiveness*. Alexandria, Virginia: Institute for Defence Analysis.

Curcione, N. (1997) 'Suburban Snowmen: Facilitating Factors in the Careers of Middle-Class Coke Dealers', *Deviant Behavior*, vol. 18, pp. 233-253.

Davies, A. (1998) 'Street Gangs, Crime and Policing in Glasgow During the 1930s: The Case of the Beehive Boys', *Social History*, vol. 23, no. 3, pp. 251-267.

Denton, B. and O'Malley, P. (1999) 'Gender, Trust and Business: Women Drug Dealers in an Illicit Economy', *British Journal of Criminology*, vol. 39, pp. 513-530.

DesRoches F. (1999) *Wholesale Drug Dealers*, paper presented to panel on 'The Structure and Operation of Illegal Commodity Markets', Annual Meeting of the American Society of Criminology, Toronto, November 1999.

Dorn, N., Murji, K. and South, N. (1992) *Traffickers: Drug Markets and Law Enforcement*. London: Routledge.

Dorn, N., Oette, L. and White, S. (1998) 'Drugs Importation and the Bifurcation of Risk: Capitalization, Cut Outs and Organized Crime', *British Journal of Criminology*, vol. 38, pp. 537-560.

Dunlap, E., Johnson, B. and Manwar, A. (1994) 'A Successful Female Crack Dealer: Case Study of a Deviant Career', *Deviant Behavior*, vol. 15, pp. 1-25.

Edmunds, M., Hough, M. and Urquia, N. (1996) *Tackling Local Drug Markets*. Crime Detection and Prevention Series, Paper 80. London: Home Office.

Fagan, J. (1989) 'The Social Organisation of Drug Use and Drug Dealing Among Urban Gangs', *Criminology*, vol. 27, pp. 633-669.

Furstenburg, M. (1969) *Violence in Organised Crime*. Staff Report to the National Commission on the Causes and Prevention of Violence. Washington, DC: US Government Publishing Office.

Gambetta, D. (1988) 'Fragments of an Economic Theory of the Mafia', *Archives Europeenes de Sociologie*, vol. 29, pp. 127-45.

Grapendaal, M., Leuw, E. and Nelen, H. (1995) *A World of Opportunities: Lifestyle and Economic Behaviour of Heroin Addicts in Amsterdam.* New York: State University of New York Press.

Hagan, F. (1983) 'The Organised Crime Continuum: A Further Specification of a New Conceptual Model', *Criminal Justice Review,* vol. 8, pp. 52-57.

Hobbs, D. (1988) *Doing the Business: Entrepreneurship, Detectives and the Working Class in the East End of London.* Oxford: Clarendon Press.

Hobbs, D. (1995) *Bad Business: Professional Crime in Modern Britain.* Oxford: Oxford University Press.

Hobbs, D. (1997) 'Professional Crime: Change, Continuity and the Enduring Myth of the Underworld', *Sociology,* vol. 31, no. 1, pp. 57-72.

Hobbs, D. (1998) 'Going Down the Glocal: The Local Context of Organised Crime', *Howard Journal of Criminal Justice,* vol. 37, no. 4, pp. 407-422.

Hobbs, D. (2001a) 'The Firm: Organisational Logic and Criminal Culture on a Shifting Terrain', *British Journal of Criminology,* vol. 41, no. 4, pp. 549-560.

Hobbs, D. (2001b) 'Violence and Organised Crime', in Hagen, J. (Ed.), *Handbook of Violence.* Boulder, Colorado: Westview Press, forthcoming.

Ianni, A.F. and Ianni, R.E. (1990) 'Network Analysis', in Andrews, P.P. and Peterson, M.B (Eds.), *Criminal Intelligence Analysis.* Loomis, CA: Palmer Enterprises.

Ianni, F. (1972) *A Family Business. Kinship and Social Control in Organised Crime.* New York: Russell Sage Foundation.

Jacobs, B.A. (1992) 'Drugs and Deception: Undercover Infiltration and Dramaturgical Theory', *Human Relations,* vol. 45, pp. 1293-1309.

Jacobs, B.A. (1996) 'Crack Dealers and Restrictive Deterrence: Identifying Narcs', *Criminology,* vol. 34, pp. 409-431.

Jacobs, B.A. (1999) *Dealing Crack: The Social World of Streetcorner Selling.* Boston: Northeastern University Press.

Jacobs, B.A. (2000) *Robbing Drug Dealers: Violence Beyond the Law*. New York: Aldine de Gruyter.

Jefferson,T. and Carlen, P. (Eds.) (1996) *Masculinities, Social Relations and Crime*. Special issue of the *British Journal of Criminology*, vol. 36, no. 3.

Johnson, B.D., Goldstein, P.J., Preble, E., Schmeidler, J., Lipton, D.S., Spunt, B. and Miller, T. (1985) *Taking Care of Business: The Economics of Crime by Heroin Abusers*. Lexington: Lexington Books.

Johnson, B.D., Hamid, A. and Sanabria, H. (1992) 'Emerging Models of Crack Distribution', in Mieczkowski, T. (Ed.), *Drugs, Crime and Social Policy*. Boston: Allyn and Bacon.

Katz, J. (1988) *Seductions of Crime*. New York: Basic Books.

Lewis, R., Hartnoll, R., Bryer, S., Daviaud, E. and Mitcheson, M. (1985) 'Scoring Smack: The Illicit Heroin Market in London, 1980-1983', *British Journal of Addiction*, vol. 80, pp. 281-289.

Lupsha, P. (1981) 'Individual Choice, Material Culture, and Organised Crime', *Criminology*, vol. 19, pp. 3-24.

MacCoun, R. and Reuter, P. (1992) 'Are the Wages of Sin $30 an Hour? Economic Aspects of Street-Level Drug Dealing', *Crime and Delinquency*, vol. 38, pp. 477-491.

MacDonald, Z. and Pyle, D. (Eds.) (2000) *Illicit Activity. The Economics of Crime, Drugs and Tax Fraud*. Aldershot: Ashgate/Dartmouth.

Maher, L. (1997) *Sexed Work: Gender, Race and Resistance in a Brooklyn Drug Market*. Oxford: Clarendon Press.

Maltz, M. (1976) 'On Defining "Organised Crime"', *Crime and Delinquency*, vol. 22, pp. 338-346.

Maltz, M. (1985) 'Towards Defining Organised Crime', in Alexander, H. and Caiden, G. (Eds.), *The Politics and Economics of Organised Crime*. Lexington, MA: D.C. Heath.

Mieczkowski, T. (1990) 'Crack Distribution in Detroit', *Contemporary Drug Problems*, vol. 17, pp. 9-30.

Mieczkowski, T. (1994) 'The Experiences of Women Who Sell Crack: Some Descriptive Data from the Detroit Crack Ethnography Project', *Journal of Drug Issues,* vol. 24, no. 2, pp. 227-248.

Murphy, S., Waldorf, D. and Reinerman, C. (1990) 'Drifting into Dealing: Becoming a Cocaine Seller', *Qualitative Sociology,* vol. 13, pp. 321-343.

Natarajan, M. (2000) 'Understanding the Structure of a Drug Trafficking Organisation: A Conversational Analysis', in Natarajan, M. and Hough, M. (Eds.), *Illegal Drug Markets: From Research to Prevention Policy.* Monsey, NY: Criminal Justice Press.

Natarajan, M. and Belanger, M. (1998) 'Varieties of Upper-Level Drug Dealing Organisations: A Typology of Cases Prosecuted in New York City', *Journal of Drug Issues,* vol. 28, no. 4, pp. 1005-1026.

Natarajan, M. and Hough, M. (Eds.). (2000) *Illegal Drug Markets: From Research to Prevention Policy.* Monsey, NY: Criminal Justice Press.

Natarajan, M., Clarke, R.V. and Johnson, B.D. (1995) 'Telephones as Facilitators of Drug Dealing: A Research Agenda', *European Journal on Criminal Policy and Research,* vol. 3, no. 3, pp. 137-153.

National Criminal Intelligence Service (2000) 'United Kingdom Drug Prices', *Nexus,* issue no. 9, Autumn 2000, p. 17.

Ovenden, C., Loxley, W. and Mcdonald, C. (1995) *The West Australian Drug Market: Descriptions from Convicted Drug Dealers, 1992.* National Centre for Research into the Prevention of Drug Abuse, Curtin University of Technology.

Pearson, G. (1990) 'Drugs, Law Enforcement and Criminology', in Berridge, V. (Ed.), *Drugs Research and Policy in Britain: A Review of the 1980s.* Aldershot: Avebury.

Pearson, G. (1991) 'Drug-Control Policies in Britain', in Tonry, M. (Ed.), *Crime and Justice: A Review of Research,* vol. 14. Chicago: Chicago University Press.

Pearson, G. (1993) 'Varieties of Ethnography: Limits and Possibilities in the Field of Illegal Drug Use', in Garretsen, H.F.L., van de Goor, L.A.M., Kaplan, C.D., Korf, D.J., Spruit, I.P. and de Zwart, W.M. (Eds.), *Illegal Drug Use: Research Methods for Hidden Populations.* Rotterdam: Netherlands Institute on Alcohol and Drugs.

Pearson, G. (2001) 'Normal Drug Use: Ethnographic Fieldwork Among an Adult Network of Recreational Drug Users in Inner London', *Substance Use and Misuse,* vol. 36, no., 1, pp. 167-200.

Polsky, N. (1967) *Hustlers, Beats, and Others.* New York: Aldine.

Polsky, N. (1998) *Hustlers, Beats, and Others.* (Expanded edition). New York: Lyon Press.

Power, R. (1989) 'Participant Observation and Its Place in the Study of Illicit Drug Abuse', *British Journal of Addiction,* vol. 84, pp. 43-52.

Power, R., Green, A., Poster, R. and Stimson, G. (1995) 'A Qualitative Study of the Purchasing and Distribution Patterns of Cocaine and Crack Users in England and Wales', *Addiction Research,* vol. 2, no. 4, pp. 363-379.

Preble, E. and Casey, J.J. (1969) 'Taking Care of Business: The Heroin User's Life on the Street', *International Journal of the Addictions,* vol. 4, no. 1, pp. 1-24.

Reuter, P. (1983) *Disorganised Crime.* Cambridge, Mass.: MIT Press.

Reuter, P. (2000) 'Transnational Crime: Drug Smuggling'. Conference on Transnational Crime, University of Cambridge, January 2000.

Reuter, P. and Hagga, J. (1989) *The Organization of High-Level Drug Markets: An Exploratory Study.* Santa Monica: RAND.

Reuter, P. and Kleiman, M.A. (1986) 'Risks and Prices: An Economic Analysis of Drug Enforcement', in Tonry, M. and Morris, N. (Eds.), *Crime and Justice: A Review of Research,* vol. 7. Chicago: Chicago University Press.

Reuter, P., MacCoun, R. and Murphy, P. (1990) *Money from Crime: A Study of the Economics of Drug Dealing in Washington D.C.* Santa Monica: RAND.

Ruggiero, V. (1996) *Organised and Corporate Crime in Europe.* Aldershot: Dartmouth.

Samuel, R. (1981) *East End Underworld: Chapters in the Life of Arthur Harding.* London: Routledge and Kegan Paul.

Shover, N. (1996) *Great Pretenders: Pursuits and Careers of Persistent Thieves.* Boulder, Colorado: Westview Press.

Sparrow, M. (1991) 'The Application of Network Analysis to Criminal Intelligence: An Assessment of the Prospects', *Social Networks,* vol. 13, no. 3, pp. 251-274.

Tunnell, K. (1993) 'Inside the Drug Trade: Trafficking from the Dealer's Perspective', *Qualitative Sociology,* vol. 16, pp. 361-381.

Uzzi, B. (1997) 'Social Structure and Competition in Interfirm Networks: The Paradox of Embeddedness', *Administrative Science Quarterly,* vol. 42, pp. 35-67.

VanNostrand, L.M. and Tewksbury, R. (1999) 'The Motives and Mechanics of Operating an Illegal Drug Enterprise', *Deviant Behavior,* vol. 20, pp. 57-83.

Wagstaff, A. and Maynard, A. (1988) *Economic Aspects of the Illicit Drug Market and Drug Enforcement Policies in the United Kingdom.* Home Office Research Study no. 95. London: HMSO.

Ward, J. and Pearson, G. (1997) 'Recreational Drug Use and Drug Dealing in London: An Ethnographic Study', in Korf, D. and Riper, H. (Eds.), *Illicit Drug Use in Europe.* Amsterdam: University of Amsterdam.

Wasserman, S. and Faust, K. (1994) *Social Network Analysis: Methods and Applications.* Cambridge: Cambridge University Press.

Williams, P. (1993) 'Transnational Crime Organisations and National Security', *Survival,* vol. 36, pp. 96-113.

Williams, T. (1989) *The Cocaine Kids.* New York: Addison Wesley.

Williams, T., Dunlap, E., Johnson, B.D. and Hamid, A. (1992) 'Personal Safety in Dangerous Places', *Journal of Contemporary Ethnography,* vol. 21, no. 3, pp. 343-74.

Woodiwiss, M. (1993) 'Crime's Global Reach', in Pearce, F. and Woodiwiss, M. (Eds.), *Global Crime Connections.* Basingstoke: Macmillan.

Wright, R. T. and Decker, S.H. (1997) *Armed Robbers in Action: Stickups and Street Culture.* Boston: Northeastern University Press.

RDS Publications

Requests for Publications

Copies of our publications and a list of those currently available may be obtained from:

Home Office
Research, Development and Statistics Directorate
Communications Development Unit
Room 201, Home Office
50 Queen Anne's Gate
London SW1H 9AT
Telephone: 020 7273 2084 (answerphone outside of office hours)
Facsimile: 020 7222 0211
E-mail: publications.rds@homeoffice.gsi.gov.uk

alternatively

why not visit the RDS website at
        Internet: http://www.homeoffice.gov.uk/rds/index.html

where many of our publications are available to be read on screen or downloaded for printing.